warriors' war

HEALING THE BATTLE WITH TRAUMA AND PTSD

warriors' war

HEALING THE BATTLE WITH TRAUMA AND PTSD

The real war is to heal your heart,

A WARRIORS' WAR

MATTHEW BRUCE

the kind press

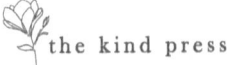

Copyright © 2020 Matthew Bruce
First published by the kind press, 2020

All rights reserved. No part of this book may be reproduced, stored in a retrieval system or transmitted in any form or by any means, electronic, mechanical photocopying, recording, or otherwise, without written permission from the author and publisher.

The author of this book does not dispense medical advice or prescribe the use of any technique as a form of treatment for physical, emotional, or medical problems without the advice of a physician, either directly or indirectly. The intent of the author is only to offer information of a general nature to help you in your quest for wellbeing. While the publisher and author have used their best efforts in preparing this book, the material in this book is of the nature of general comment only. In the event you use any of the information in this book for yourself, the author and the publisher assume no responsibility for your actions.

Cover and interior design by Elle Lynn

Cataloguing-in-Publication entry is available from the National Library Australia.

NATIONAL LIBRARY OF AUSTRALIA

ISBN 978-0-6487927-3-4 (Paperback)

ISBN 978-0-6487927-6-5 (Ebook)

I would like to dedicate this book to Ruth Balcke.
There are not many hearts that walk this earth that are as soft,
gentle and unconditional as yours. Without your heart
showing me the way, I would still be lost and disconnected.
My beloved.

acknowledgements

To anyone who is healing from any form of trauma, my heart goes out to you. We all have a story and odds are if you are reading this you have or know someone with PTSD. I want to personally acknowledge you for your battles, your challenges and your wins. May we all make healthy choices and grow our capacity to love ourselves and others.

Contents

acknowledgements   *vii*
preface   *xi*

part one

chapter one	work	3
chapter two	men's work is powerful	13
chapter three	master your mind	21
chapter four	fight-or-flight	27
chapter five	the present moment	39
chapter six	emotional stress	49
chapter seven	physical stress	55
chapter eight	environmental stress	59
chapter nine	nutritional stress	63

part two

chapter ten	yoga	71
chapter eleven	nourishment and self-love	75
chapter twelve	visualisation	89
chapter thirteen	breathwork	93
chapter fourteen	journaling	101
chapter fifteen	sound healing	103
chapter sixteen	energy healing	107
chapter seventeen	yoga qi gong	111

part three

chapter eighteen	outside world	119
chapter nineteen	inside world	127
chapter twenty	patterns of the past	141
chapter twenty-one	for the partners	149
chapter twenty-two	social responsibility	155
chapter twenty-three	shame	167
chapter twenty-four	embodiment	173

afterword   *179*
thriving warriors   *181*
about the author   *183*

preface

The place is called rock bottom. You may know it, perhaps even been there yourself. It's a place of suffering where you feel more broken and defeated than most people could ever imagine. You give up, the hopeless stream of suicidal thoughts within your mind doesn't stop. Often when we become so addicted to recreating the past, we put ourselves into deadly situations—time and time again—just to feel alive, to feel *anything*. We disconnect from feeling human. The disconnection we create becomes a downward spiral for years and years, and we don't consciously even know it. This detached feeling can seem like our norm, as we do anything to numb, forget, bury, rid ourselves from the pain in our hearts. That's a glimpse into the world of someone suffering from post-traumatic stress disorder—PTSD.

That's a glimpse into *my* story, *my* pain. I've been addicted to drugs, sleeping pills, binge drinking, sex, and lying to myself and others. Yet, I soldiered on and put on a brave face. That was the training and how I was conditioned to do life—to disconnect further and to keep moving forward—to react to life rather than respond. The only problem was I was moving in the wrong direction. I was going backwards and suffering and my reaction to cope was through *disconnection.*

I was the enemy and at war with my own heart. Every moment I fuelled the pain, I would slip further. I was in denial that I needed help and denial that my behaviour was a problem. In every aspect of life I was a pretender.

I could look people in the eye and say, 'I'm OK,' or 'I'm good.'

Lie! I wasn't good.

I was struggling and well on the way to becoming another statistic of PTSD. Another brainwashed, brain-damaged soldier who gave the better part of his life away. Returning scared and damaged from a fight that was not his. We fought wars based on messages and foundations of false terror, only to complete timeless cycles of bringing the scars home and inflicting them on loved ones and furthermore to ourselves.

To anyone who has ever stood in my pain as I project this, thank you. Thank you for your courage, faith, love and support through the times I wasn't myself. Looking back, I'm not sorry, though. As I now see the pain as a blessing. A blessing which fuels the fire within me to allow change for myself and my fellow brothers of war. As you see, we men are experts at hiding our emotions and how we truly feel. This is not because we don't want to feel, but because of the lifetimes of pain we have inherited in our male lineage that has locked our hearts down. I am not a sufferer from PTSD—I was—but I choose to never look back or identify with that label, ever again. I'm now thriving, living my life with balance as a grounded man, anchored within and here to help others.

FOR EVERY SECOND WE STAND IN THE STORY OF THE PAST, WE LIMIT OUR FUTURE.

For every second we stand in the label of being broken, we are broken. We are limitless to what we can achieve if we have the fire within to do so. I am here standing before you today with my heart open and my arms wide, to share my wounds and pain and my journey. I hope it may help my brothers and their partners who are suffering.

The current medical system is also broken and is in a sad state. I have sat in front of leading doctors within their fields, openly admitting that the textbook treatments do not work. My whole life I've known that I am a problem-solver. Yet, I was not entirely sure what problem I was meant to solve and what that message looked like to spread. I now know it's helping my brothers return home to their hearts from battle. So, men and women—the feminine and the masculine—can live together in peace and thrive once again. This book is a devotion to heal from pain holistically and from the heart space. The secret to healing is held by your loved ones. Through our relationships and the act of love for others, you can find love again for yourself.

As males, we have become disconnected from the healthy *Warrior* that once lived in harmony with nature. In today's society, the modern man is showing constant displays of anger and unhealthy behaviours, he isn't respecting masculinity, or women, and this is a problem spanning the whole earth. When did we lose this connection we hold so dear to honour and respect our body, mind and soul? *Is the answer, war?*

For many, many years, the men who've walked this planet have been sent to battle time and time again. Returning more broken each time, bringing the battle home to our primary relationships. We then pass on these same scars to the women or loved ones and shape our younger generations to become more disconnected from their feelings. The time for change is upon us with a wave of men stepping into healthy versions of masculinity. Men are realising the self-help phenomenon sweeping the globe is not just for women. These are fascinating times to be alive, to see a new level of direction within males taking place. A time that is less about sporting ability and body image, and more about mindful-based living.

In reading this book, you will find visualisations and other awareness-based techniques to assist you to heal from the inside out. I have seen first-hand how powerful these techniques are, and I'm excited to share them with you. It doesn't matter what state or behaviour you are in, following the holistic approaches in this book will help you breakthrough any resistance to change your story, your life. You can create the limitless version of you that has always existed.

For as long as we can trace back our family bloodlines, we have participated in some form of war. And by no fault of their own, the men who have returned from those wars have been broken and returned scared and feeling unsafe in their bodies. This has slowly contributed to building a global culture of unhealthy masculinity. I've seen men shut down their emotions and cannot utilise their natural ability to shift the traumas they've witnessed in battle. Should you not have been to war, you too, have indirectly inherited the struggle over the lifetimes on this planet. The pain and suffering in war extends beyond men and includes women too.

For centuries women have witnessed and suffered the atrocities of battle. I wonder how much of this pain has been passed down to you. We're seeing men lie to their partners as they've lost the vulnerability to admit personal truth. These truths run deep, they are deeply connected to the wounds of the past and present. We dared to march off to war time and time again, yet now we don't dare to be honest to ourselves or loved ones. These patterns are consuming relationships and controlling interactions with loved ones. We can change the behaviours of this modern society. It may seem like a lifetime away for some, yet the change and results are much closer than you probably know.

A healthy, limitless lifetime with no attachment to the past or trauma awaits. Once we realise the power of making healthy choices in this present moment, we hold the key to healing and changing any behaviour.

With lifetimes of war men have inherited and continue to feel fear, shame, judgment and rejection, we're protecting our hearts at any cost. Some may view this as a birthright, inherited from the past and shaping the current state of masculinity. We are completely disconnected from the harmony we achieved in ancient times; our society has slipped from the peace of our Indigenous Australian ancestors. Even though we didn't choose this conditioning, we do have the choice to limit its impact on future generations and on our current relationships, and to dissolve the pain that carries on in our hearts.

So, how do we heal and move past our conditioning? The answer is by finding the way back to your heart; the heart knows the way to healthy leadership, love, masculinity and how to restore the balance of harmony in the modern world we live today. This takes time, work and a desire to want to *change*. The road back to heart is no easy path travelled. It can seem painful, scary, and worse than any war ever experienced. As you heal, your heart and ability to feel the pain of yesterday grows. This might come as quite a shock when you explore your emotions as opposed to suppressing them. Yet in this pain, we receive a gift. The ability to feel the love from the heart and this is the gift we then give to others—*love*. To live from a place of expansive love, you will become renewed and flourish once you peel back the layers of pain. You also mend the wounds passed down by any ancestors and unlock the incredible potential within, and you heal. If your intention to improve is pure, you will be rewarded beyond your wildest dreams. Once we live from a place of *alignment*, our whole life falls into place. When you choose love for yourself—and do the work to heal your heart—purpose, passion, and abundance are just a few of the by-products you'll receive.

For years I was disconnected, my heart closed. I was wandering in a lost state of existence: abusing drugs, alcohol, food, and women. Yet mostly, I was harming myself. *Am I just another victim of war?* I thought. I was at a low point with an even lower self-worth; I chose to be angry with the world every day. Yes, that's correct, *I chose*. Deep within, I was making the choice. You see, happiness is a choice and so is anger. Anger can be so deeply buried within that we are not even aware that we are holding on to the pain. I was completely in denial and not even aware of the scars that being in the Army placed on me, and how it was affecting my lifestyle and *all* my relationships. My self-opinion was so low that I would continuously subject my mind and body to a cycle of continuous torture over and over. I wondered if these were the effects of PTSD, or was it that all my male colleagues were behaving this way?

I still question to this day how I felt so broken and yet could still function in everyday society. To the world, perhaps my behaviour was just that of another male, you know, the 'men behaving like men' mindset. Fortunately for me, this cycle grew to a point where I could not deny the pain within and my desperate need for change arrived. For every act of *not* showing up for myself, my disconnection worsened. The need to escape my life increased with every memory of my past. One thing I learnt was that every day I spent living an unhealthy lifestyle, I increased the damage to my heart and health.

Our health and wellbeing are directly related to the current state of our emotional past. Every day we spend in the cycles of our emotional patterns from the past we become numb, more disconnected and more unloved. The cycle for me fuelled itself to the point where I didn't know myself and was, in turn, looking for anything to know and feel I was alive. I was always lying to my partner, using drugs and literally self-destructing from the inside out. All I wanted was to be loved, not a love from someone else but a love from myself. Yet my world and internal perception were so warped that I could not see what was present the whole time. I was hurt, angry and disconnected.

I was at war with my heart. I question if the disconnection I buried in my heart was the reason I left for the Army in the first place. Nevertheless, at my lowest point a miracle occurred. I forged a desire to choose growth in every moment. In my willingness to change, I used some simple techniques which I will show you in this book to step away from bad habits and to create a healthier version of you. Before writing this book, I had only read a handful of books. The very thought of writing a book would be something that an older version of me would have laughed at. However, once we have a *desire* to *change*; anything is possible. This book is a testament to that *change*.

I've often questioned in reflection where this trend of not connecting with my feelings came from. Was it passed down from my grandfather to my father to me? I had to tap into my problem-solving nature; it was time to use this natural gift and logic on myself. I knew it was time to understand where the problem began. Yet when we explore the history of humanity, we can see that it is littered with war, violence and depression. When I reflected on previous generations, it allowed me to have a higher level of compassion and forgiveness for the loved ones within my family. Learning to forgive was a great place to start healing.

Through this book, we will explore the ability to forgive ourselves and the male lineage that has created the unhealthy world we live in today. To stand in front of someone you have hurt and take full responsibility and say you have corrected your behaviour is powerful. And the only way we can do this is by having compassion for ourselves and for our loved ones. The empathy for the other person then overrides any self-interest that may hold you back from speaking this truth. When taking responsibility and speaking from a place of radical truth, we will help transform the world to be a better place. This power will help you in every aspect of your life through healing the past to transforming your future relationships.

When I reflect on what I put my mind and body through as a soldier, I feel compassionate for the younger version of me. The amount of suicide that we see post-military is a real indicator of the amount of stress and damage we have endured. The world is a highly stimulating place as it is. With the pace of modern society, our minds are being placed under large amounts of stress every day. It's this very state of the world that needs to change before we can truly heal from our past traumas. Yet we can create a new relationship and a new way to interact with the world, one that helps us heal from our past trauma and instils a growth mindset. We may feel like we're only one fish in a gigantic ocean and that we won't make a difference, but we can take radical responsibility for how we show up. In us embodying this new healthy power we can create changes within our relationships and place an end to the many wounds we have inherited from battles of the past.

I look back now and can see I was so scared of love. Younger versions of me existed that did not want to hug other people or receive intimacy on deeper levels. My heart was scared it would go through the pain of being rejected, and my connection to the world worsened every day. It's a confronting realisation to understand that much of our life has been shaped by our unconscious behaviour. I have inherited many basic patterns and human behaviours from other lifetimes of battles and possibly my grandfather serving in WWII.

I used to have issues even hugging people. It made me uncomfortable and I'd feel awkward, even hugging good friends I'd known for years would still make me feel this way. As males, we can sometimes build walls so high to protect us from the past. This was not a choice I was making as I was genuinely unaware of these interactions or did not have the emotional intelligence at the time to correct this. Yet in my desire to change, this was one of the first things that had to go. I remember being on a holiday with my mother and consciously choosing to lean in, hug her and tell her I loved her. I was breaking the cycle within our family. Giving her the words she longed for as a child from her father. Such a small gesture of choosing to hug your family can go a long way to heal and assist breaking down past traumas, allowing us to grow as males. Should you be reading this, and your loved ones may have passed, you can still hold them in your heart. Should your wounds be bound to that of a fallen friend or comrade in battle, we can find ways to heal and move past this suffering. To recover from any trauma, past patterns or PTSD, we must learn to feel and embrace our emotions. Reconnecting with our family is a great place to start.

I wrote *Warriors' War* with the intention of assisting my brothers to heal from trauma. Together we can rise above the unhealthy masculine. Should you not identify with trauma or unhealthy behaviour yet still feel called to read this book, you are also on the right path.

I also wrote it to give women an understanding of the pain and suffering men hold. These past traumatic experiences that I speak of are shaping our every word, interaction, and relationship we are having. Every time we get angry, feel disconnected, act in toxic ways, we are hurting. It is never a reflection of the women in our relationships, yet we are sometimes not capable of feeling and expressing the pain in our hearts. Through lifetimes of battles, we have disconnected. These past experiences act like layers on our heart as we build protection from a very early age. We are not only protecting our hearts from this lifetime yet from all the wounds before us that still need to be healed. The unresolved trauma from past and present has us living in a survival mode. The holistic steps that will unfold in this book are collected from my direct healing experiences and have helped shape the man that I am today. In taking responsibility, I could change the way I was interacting with the world around me.

THROUGH FOCUSING ON THE PRESENT MOMENT, WE CAN MOVE FORWARD ONE STEP AT A TIME.

Responsibility for our thoughts, words and actions is a large part of moving forward from trauma and healing our hearts. We can influence our thoughts, which can change our words and actions. Healing is a choice and one that you are currently in the process of just by reading this book.

By changing our personal story, we can truly see the world through a new set of eyes. Ask yourself, do you sit with the terrible pain and memories of the past? Or do you do the work and free yourself of this pain? You may sit there and feel that you are healthy and have nothing to heal and work on. If you can sit down in your backyard for one hour without looking at your phone and feel joy in your heart, you are doing a great job in life. If you can't find the joy or bliss in the simple things in life or need a cigarette or a beer to feel this level of joy, I invite you to read on.

Change takes time, commitment, tears, anger and effort. Immense happiness in life is awaiting you in every moment. We have endless potential in this life if we take action and make a change to move forward from the conditioning and behaviour we have inherited.

We are part of an evolution where mankind can grow and invite healthy change into our daily lives. By acceptance and action, we are creating a future where men can openly discuss how they are feeling. This is potent stuff. By creating a space where men can share publicly from a place of truth, we have the potential to change the whole world. Through speaking our truth and being our true authentic self, we will be the catalyst for change.

WHEN WE SPEAK OUR TRUTH AND OPEN OUR HEART TO THE PAST, WE HAVE THE POWER TO HEAL FROM ANY WOUND.

I want women who read this book to understand, support and encourage their partners to share his emotions deeply and openly. It is a beautiful moment within a relationship when we can share honestly, and women have a vital role to play too. Should a man be brave enough to open up and communicate these deep feelings, she must meet him with compassion and understanding. Should they be deemed as unnecessary or looked upon with rejection, they could trigger the same trauma that created the negative patterns from the past.

So, women, your role is vital in guiding men back to their heart. The effort will be rewarded as your upgraded male will hold space for you in return. Together you will share a deeper level of love and respect for one another as you both understand your love and wounds on a deeper level. Remember, when your partner is leaning in to choose love and growth, what could appear to be like a normal behaviour to you, could be an extreme amount of effort on his part. Men, in saying that, if you feel your partner isn't receiving you, communicate with her some more.

Healing is powerful. You will hold space and allow another brother, father, or son to share their pain openly too. This will allow for a vast amount of change to occur within our world. Through this shift, we will establish a new world where men and women can act from a healthy place. Not always understood, not always in alignment, and not always flawless, but improving and shifting the momentum towards a better world. We live in an age where the time is now to speak from our heart, not our mind.

I would like to give thanks to any teacher, guide, friend, enemy, or loved one on this path. I see you, and I thank you for sharing this path to change. For all the women in my life that I have ever caused pain and suffering to, I apologise. At times, I was just a sad boy in desperate need of love. In need of love from myself. I know that now. I am incredibly grateful for all the interactions and experiences I have had in my life to this point. I have shifted my perception, taken responsibility, and the world looks and feels amazing. I look back and reflect on the past with acceptance and understanding.

As you use the activities in this book, you will free yourself from the judgments of the past and will look forward in every situation with optimism and a sense of relief. If we do the work, we can leave the past behind with forgiveness and compassion.

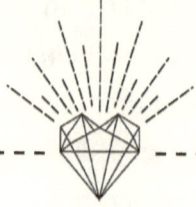

Before we begin...

Healing requires action and an idea or desire to change is the first step. Healing can be as simple as closing our eyes and visualising 'who we want to be', we then 'take action' to fill in the blanks. Diet, self-love, healthy relationships, movement, reflection, responsibility; these are a small portion of the blanks we must fill in to achieve that vision. Just one healthy choice at a time is all it takes to heal.

Wherever you are, find a quiet place and simply close your eyes and envision a future version of yourself... make it real and feel into your environment in that moment.
Picture yourself with a smile and a deep knowing in your heart that you are already healed.
Hold this vision within in your mind and let it go.
Try this activity every morning and night. The more you practice this simple visualisation, the quicker and easier your healing will manifest.

chapter one
work

CPL MATTHEW BRUCE OF THE ROYAL AUSTRALIAN ARMY. That was my title, my work, who I was. Where it *all* began.

In 2014, they exposed me to extremely graphic digital material. I was working on a highly classified deployment in Jordan that focused on foreign countries monitoring social media of the terrorist organisation, the Islamic State (ISIS). I did not have the emotional intelligence to understand what this exposure to graphic material was doing to my body and mind back then. In reflection, I don't believe the Australian Army did either.

On my return from Jordan, I visited the base doctor. He asked if I was feeling okay after watching the countless beheadings and human suffering. I was working in an unhealthy environment where I'd been suppressing my feelings for years. To be honest, I wasn't even sure what that question really meant. *Are you okay?* I mean, if I looked around to the role models within my unit, I would follow their lead, bury my feelings, and get on with the next job.

So, I replied, "I am feeling good."

At that point, I'd been an Australian soldier for nine years and was currently posted to and deployed with the Australia Special Air Service Regiment in Perth. In my position as a communications technician, I was to establish and provide communications for some Australian intelligence soldiers between a US base and the Australia embassy in Amman, Jordan.

Looking back on the six-month deployment, I could recognise some significant changes in my personality and in my relationship with my partner at the time, Alicia. I became more distant and reduced the regularity of my usual phone calls and conversations. On other deployments to Afghanistan, I still wanted to phone home and talk to Alicia. If I trace back, the workload and the time spent absent from Alicia in that three to four years before this deployment, it would look like just another failed 'Army distant relationship'. With an average of nine months a year spent on course, deployed or on exercises, it was any wonder our love lasted that long. I definitely was in burnout and closing my heart down on this deployment, and my partner sensed this. I'd grown distant, closed off and disconnected from my emotions and joy. I can truthfully say that writing this passage makes my eyes tear as I reflect on my relationship with Alicia, and the breakdown of the relationship with myself.

Relationships reflect of our inner world, and back then, my inner world was on a downward spiral. As you read this book, you will understand it's healthy to be vulnerable. It's healing to communicate that we are feeling less than amazing. More importantly, it is healthy to make time and space for our emotions so they can be explored and heard, honoured and accepted with gratitude and not judged as weak. As men, we have had an enormous stigma in Australia, the Military and the world for sharing our emotions. I hope that this book is part of a shifting culture where men can openly discuss their feelings and not be judged by themselves or others.

I have often discussed this with my present-day partner, Ruth, and firmly believe that the deployments to Afghanistan and Jordan were just training in war. The real war fully took hold when I returned home. Healing your heart, recovering from horrific injuries or the tragedy of a family member not making it back is the *real* war. This level of trauma compounds the struggles in life we have already absorbed from the past. This is where a real warrior is born by coming home and healing their heart and showing a deep level of love to their family, brothers and community. To go back and unpack lifetimes of war and disconnection within our heart is courage. To heal our traumatic past, we must find the uncomfortable parts of our inner world and lean into that discomfort. Leaning into our edge allows us to free ourselves from the very memory or attachment that creates the resistance of anything other than joy. I can't emphasise this enough: the discomfort we feel in life is what we must feel for growth and healing. Should you be afraid to be seen or feel anxious in certain situations—this is where you must explore.

My opinion has changed lately, and I view any 9-5 job in the world as high stress. Yes, even a 38-hour week at Kmart is too much! It does not allow for enough rest, enough connection. Humanity is on the edge of a massive collapse, and depression and anxiety are leading the way. Shortly after my time in the Army, I worked in a large mining company and I found this corporate environment further damaging to my health. I take full responsibility that I was suffering from PTSD at this establishment, and this could be witnessed in my anger and relationships with co-workers. Though, I was not alone as many managers were having physical health problems. I was constantly looking for negativity in the workplace. This was part of the conditioning I'd received from my time in the Army. This outward focus was hard-wired into my makeup for survival, yet it was only meant to be activated when under threat, like in the Army. I was so conditioned to high levels of stimulation from the Army and I brought this to my new career.

**WE'RE WIRED AND CONDITIONED TO LOOK FOR STRESS IN THE WORKPLACE.
WE'RE LOOKING AT THE WORLD LIKE WE ARE IN SOME FORM OF DANGER.**

This level of stimulation limits our ability to communicate with our natural intelligence and logic. I could not see the workplace for what it *was* and continually focused on the negative. I saw it as a threat because it felt comfortable and wouldn't give me the level of stress I was addicted to. This is not an environment that will allow us to heal. Unfortunately, the human mind can interpret the current world as a constant threat. In this threat mindset, we lose a very fundamental level of internal communication. As our attention is so outwardly focused, we forget about our inner world. Also, we look to coping mechanisms like coffee and other sugar-based foods to assist the stimulation and limit our internal communication.

I couldn't understand my trauma and attachment to the past while I was working in a 9-5 office job. The stress on my body compounded from all the conditioning I received in the Army. In saying that, I could create a lot of change in my behaviour before I left through using tools like meditation and changing my diet. When I incorporated these new habits into my life, I healed, slowly. I was actively choosing to be aware of my behaviour and asked myself the tough questions. The more time and energy we give our *self*, the more we will grow, and the benefits be seen.

At the time of my deployment to Jordan, I was a highly functioning soldier in the Australian SASR, fuelled on adrenalin, six cups of black American coffee a day and extreme workouts. It's a wonder I have any adrenalin left in my body. I was stuck in a destructive pattern of waking up triggered by an alarm and going to bed on my phone. Every day was filled with tasks based on fear and lots of what-ifs. I received glowing reports on my deployment from both officers. My captain on this trip is, at the time of writing this book, the local Federal Liberal member for Canning. I would often observe the behaviour of my leaders and take notice of their reactions in detail. I greatly respected my leaders. Not just for their sandy beret (qualified SASR soldier) but for their leadership style and the approachability. Yet, I'd often watch their reaction to seeing a human life being taken and wonder why our responses differed.

EVERYONE IS DIFFERENT, TRAUMA EFFECTS US *ALL* IN UNIQUE WAYS.

During my time, a Jordanian pilot from the Royal Jordan Airforce crashed his plane in Syria. Two things from this incident blew me away. First, that we were in a highly classified intelligence compound in the country of Jordan and we heard the news *first* via CNN TV. It was a real show of the times, and why this task force even existed. The pilot was alive and captured by ISIS fighters in the Syrian stronghold of Alraka. Second, the Jordanian King retaliated to this news by bombing non-military targets in Syria. I can specifically remember a massive show of force from the Royal Jordanian Airforce fly overhead to attack women and children in the days that followed. Later that evening, our vehicle participated in a pro-Jordan motorcade on our return to base. It was strange to see a country uniting in this manner under these circumstances.

A video was later posted on the internet of the Jordanian pilot being burnt alive in a cage in 'High' definition footage. I apologise if this picture is triggering in any way. At the time, of watching this video, I could feel the emotion and sensations within my body. To this day I have never witnessed something as horrific. My heart goes out to soldiers and servicemen of all types and the ISIS fighters that found themselves in this tragic situation. For all the emergency service personnel, thank you for your service. The level of stress and trauma witnessed in your fields of duty is considerable, and largely unacknowledged by the broader population. I could not even begin to understand what it must feel like to show up like that *every* day. The world truly needs brave people like them.

When returning home from this deployment, my life felt like it was turned upside down. Within a matter of weeks, Alicia wanted to end our relationship. I lost the only coping mechanism I had because of injury. I turned to alcohol to further disconnect from my emotions. To make matters worse, I was asked to leave the Army after a drunken weekend found me in the possession of an illegal substance. I was by no means in an emotionally stable place to leave. Yet the Army was not too apologetic in tearing my life apart then showing me the door. To be honest, at the time when I left that Army, I had a very low emotional intelligence. I could not understand my feelings, it was either anger or a watered-down version of happiness. So, off I went on to the next chapter in my life.

Often, as they train us to disconnect and react day in and day out, we lose touch. The level of disconnection is the very reason

PTSD exists as we become stuck and fixated on trauma as we cannot process further emotions. The way I coped after leaving was the only way I knew how, through a mixture of excessive exercise, drugs, sex, food, cigarettes, porn. Anything I could find to detach I'd accept with open arms. I look back with compassion how poorly I was relating to my outside and inner worlds. To some, my behaviour may just look like a big weekend for the average Australian male. Once we remove our trauma and past wounds, this is no way to live our lives. To understand what is acutely driving our wants and needs to cope in this way is necessary to heal. Once we remove our trauma, we begin to heal and understand why we are behaving the way we do. We gain emotional intelligence and can observe our problems and behaviour in healthier ways.

OBSERVING OUR BEHAVIOUR IS THE FIRST STEP TO CHANGING IT, LABEL IT AS *HELPFUL*, OR *NOT HELPFUL*.

On the path of healing, I discovered a hidden anger within me. I projected this anger on so many layers of my life. If I listened in meditation, I could hear it, feel it, experience it. A rage that would fill my body and mind and take control when the right environmental trigger would occur. Now, I look back at this anger with celebration. Because of the destruction and adverse effects it was having on my life, it pushed me to go deeper, to understand my pain and how to change my life.

As we look forward in life, it is only our past projections that make us feel resistance. This resistance can seem like a touchy topic with our partner or struggles at work. These situations can stir emotions such as anger, fear, anxiety or judgment. We must take responsibility for our past and not project these from our inner world to our outer world. Our anger is ours to own. It is on us as men to look deep within. If we are tired or feeling depleted, the anger is still ours to own. Being hungover or stressed at work is no one's fault but our own. We should take responsibility to present ourselves to the world in a full and present capacity. This could be as easy as a morning daily practice you develop or taking time for out when you are feeling depleted.

The small healthy choices I have made to date have corrected countless unhealthy behaviours within me and improved my life beyond what words can express. I'm still a work in progress, looking forward to what I can observe in the next present moment.

Often our thoughts are present and are creating our feelings and actions in the blink of an eye! Our ability to catch our thoughts and silence them in the moment is a superpower and something that takes practice. This is something I have worked with and has helped me immensely.

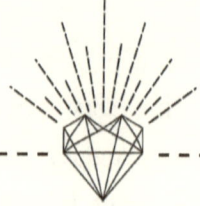

ACTIVITY: WITNESS THE STORY

Take five minutes.
Find a quiet place, close your eyes.
Breathe deeply into your belly thirty times, then sit in silence.

Ensure you are comfortable and peaceful. Laying down is an option.

As a thought pattern arises, look at it as the witness like you are not in the story, you are the observer, and label your thoughts as helpful or not helpful.
Then let it go!

This is a cognitive function we can then take into our daily life. Labelling our thoughts as not useful breaks the patterns and stop them in their tracks before they create a feeling or even worse an action.

Should you be stuck in a story, go for a walk, take some deep exhalations, put on some music, any simple action to change your state of mind will help you take back control of your not useful thoughts!
Good Luck.

chapter two
men's work is powerful

When we are around other groups of men we come back to our roots. We come back to a time and place where we can be in harmony with what is. I'm not talking about the footy with the boys, drinking beers. I'm talking about a group of men who have come together intending to support one another in a growth mindset. That can take many forms and we see these forms popping up all over the world in many cities. Every Wednesday I hang around a bunch of men at a breakfast catch up in Perth, Western Australia.

We often meet *before* the meeting for some yoga or breathwork and then head to the cafe. The power of being around a group of men like this is so uplifting and has been part of my deep healing practice. In our service we can form many unhealthy masculine relationships and behaviours, this can be because of behaviours established generations before us. In saying that, we can also form healthy ones too. So, what exactly is the voodoo that goes on in a men's circle that is so powerful? Free expression and open ears, a freedom to express your issues or achievements. We all have a deep desire and need to be seen and heard in an intimate capacity and not judged.

This is often something we are *not* experiencing in our modern world and it is something that is making this work so powerful. Often as we share, we build trust with other men on levels perhaps not experienced in our lives before. As we express deeply and more freely, we build deeper trust outwards into our community. We also witness something deeply uplifting when we express, we are all on similar paths and working through the same challenges.

I remember in one men's group I was feeling in a very low state and was having a very tough day and it was not even 8 am. When my brother shared his very similar experience, a weightlessness existed in that moment and I could smile. It was like my troubles had dissolved and shifted in an instant. I also had the opportunity to return the favour and express my truth that I was experiencing something very similar. Many people reading this may think what is the difference between this and a therapist?

I hear you and I believe our ability to express our true self with other men and women in our community is like building muscles. The more we use them, the better they become. The lack of expressing our needs and desires is one reason PTSD exists. Should we see something traumatic or be going through a tough time, our natural instinct is to bottle up our problems and suppress our truth. And in that, we are holding on to the emotion and the energy within the body. We can shift emotions in multiple ways and communicating is a very effective method.

We see that communicating in a calm, loving, respectful and attentive way is just not an option but something that feels good. We can then take our practice home to our loved ones and family members. Even better, we can take this ability to freely express emotion to our other brothers who may not to be on the path of self-growth or self-awareness.

BE THE CHANGE YOU WOULD LIKE TO SEE IN THE WORLD.

When we be the *change*, we relate to ourselves on a deeper level where we can be our true self and express our truth in every moment, regardless of who is nearby. We can do a large *body of work* to remove trauma and PTSD from our body. Yet if we don't upgrade and do the work to resolve the initial cause, we can re-accumulate emotion and energy in our body. The unhealthy culture of not expressing our emotions within a service role or first-line responder positions is part of the cause of PTSD. I feel the world is ready for this to change. This can take work! Sometimes, as we are expressing our emotions and our pain within, they can be projected as blame for another. This can look like blaming a loved one, co-workers or an organisation for the pain we are still choosing to sit in and accept.

Men's work will help you take the responsibility needed to take ownership of your internal world and how to express this in a healthy way. Men's circles have greatly assisted my ability to communicate with my partner Ruth. When we express about our own pain and realise that it has nothing to do with our lover, we are doing *the work*. To correct our patterns of behaviour and our conditioning that we have received from our parents, workplace and the world in general.

Believe me when I say this, men communicating about our feelings is the new sexy. Men doing the work is the new sexy. Who would not want to be in a relationship with a male who is doing the work to *hold* himself and then in return to *hold* his partner?

Free expression goes beyond the simple act of communicating with loved ones and men's work. Even social media can become a powerful tool to express ourselves in a healthy, loving format too. For some people, this free expression of what may be on your heart or something you have been through could be the medicine your friends need in a particular moment. There is no greater gift when we put aside our own judgement and our own comparison and just express ourselves from the heart. Men's work can take many forms, circles are just one example.

THE OLDEST TRADITIONS OF MEN'S WORK DATES BACK TO ANCIENT TRADITIONS FROM WALKABOUTS TO COMING OF AGE CEREMONIES.

The modern world has removed this work from its traditions, and it's been at a large cost. Our ability to not know our true power as men has been lost and in that we have also lost connection to wisdom and the respect for the keepers of this wisdom. We are all here to live our own life and experience it to the fullest. For thousands of years, this was refined and crafted to help hold we men. When working with other brothers, they can introduce us to healthy men and leaders who can help us embrace the darker sides of our past and help us express them. In this they hold us, and most importantly we hold ourselves on deeper levels. The deeper we can hold ourselves, the deeper we can hold our loved ones and our community.

This book is an example of that. I am here to hold you, and in this information, I am being the example of a leader as you can too. The world needs many leaders, and the time is now to step up and most importantly step into our own hearts and love ourselves deeper. There are some great examples of brothers doing the work around the world. Another brother from my local community who is a leader in deeper men's work is Tim Morrison. Tim runs some deep containers for men's work, including a program called Invictus! I have had a few brothers get amongst this work and vouch for Tim and the work that he does. I would highly recommend that you give him a follow on your page and have some healthy brother influence in your news feed.

As you can see, men's work can take many shapes and forms, there are no limitations of how this work can look and be presented. This could be your very calling to develop yourself as a male and tune in to your ability to hold other men through the lessons from your trauma and your PTSD, like I am. We all have a story; we all have a strong message. I ask you to share with me your work in the future so I can help you rise and get behind you and support you in this new healthy brotherhood. We must embrace healthy support and come from a place of supporting the new masculine through patterns of comparison and competition. Help yourself and your brothers to be their best.

This awareness of our own patterns and stories that we bring to men's groups is a large portion of the internal work we can do to grow even deeper. Often, we have not related to another group of men in such a way, and this can bring emotions up that can be witnessed and then expressed. Back to that free expression in the moment. Your expression may not be from a past pretence or about your relationship. It might be a deeper awareness within your body or thought patterns that can be expressed in the group rather than ignored, disconnected or suppressed. This is power, brother, and the deeper we understand our feelings in the moment, the quicker we can give them thanks, express and get back to our true state of joy.

I also highly recommend this work if you live in a remote part of the world too, you can still connect with groups online. I have experienced when conducting some of my first breathwork sessions in a mixed environment that I was constantly holding back sadness and some emotions I couldn't freely express. My ability to express my emotions has gone full circle and recently on a breathwork course I could express my compassion for other members on the course with tears in a healthy way. Really, these tears were connected to actions within my past and something that need to be understood and expressed. Yet as males, we can hesitate to fully lose control and release our emotions in front of women. Men's work can give you the ability to go deeper within and breakthrough that resistance or block you may hold inside.

chapter three
master your mind

One of the most significant breakthroughs I've experienced on this path was understanding that 'I create the world around me'. We are a direct representation of our *perception* and our internal worlds. Think about words. When we change our words, our perception adjusts to those set of words. This can take a little time to grasp, and firstly you will need to practice and catch yourself if you are using any negative words. I believe there is nothing more powerful than the spoken word to heal. The term itself, PTSD, is very negative and is a label we do not need to carry when we're trying to heal. The stories we tell ourselves and believe, we become. By changing our label and our stories, we can shift our mindset and the ability to live in a new way. We can introduce mantras and affirmations in our dialogue to help us shift our mindset.

Affirmations are generally written or spoken

sentences.

An example of an affirmation is: "I am feeling amazing."

All we are doing here is retraining our brain and building a new set of images for our life. This takes work! There is no magic pill to heal you, but there is a way to take control of your mind so you can build a growth mindset through mantras and affirmations. I hate to break it to you so early in the book, but no one other than *you* are here to save *you*. And like we head to the gym to train our body; we must devote time every day to retrain our brain and break the conditioning we have received from our service.

We usually say affirmations from the 'I am' perspective. This can be powerful as you are technically setting an intention in any given moment and build a new image of the future you. If we look back on history and our life, our words are very powerful. Every sentence spoken from 'I love you' to 'I hate you' holds tremendous power. Affirmations are no different. When we use affirmations, we listen, and more importantly, your subconscious mind takes note. We strengthen the story we forge.

Morning, and last thing at night, are the most powerful times to do affirmations. The subconscious mind is very impressionable, and your words will have the most effect then. I have also experimented with meditating to deep states and using affirmations like a mantra. I would repeat a few words over and over to assist the new story I was creating. In today's modern times, our minds tend toward negativity. We can correct this. For years affirmations have been incredibly powerful and allowed people to heal from multiple traumas and emotional states and even disease.

When we are living in negative thought patterns and destructive emotional states, affirmations can be flexible to target the exact problem that may be the cause. To go deeper into this subject, I would highly recommend reading *You Can Heal Your Life* by Louise Hay. She was a beautiful lady in America who mapped human emotions to illness within the body. She also created multiple affirmations to shift the emotional attachments we hold to the past. This was and still is potent healing. If we have deep emotional wounds, they can become extremely toxic to our body and mind *if* they are not acknowledged and healed.

One of the most famous affirmations in the western world is: "I am worthy." This may sound a little strange to you, yet there is a strong core belief that lives within most of us that believe we are not worthy of love. Deep within the human psyche from when we are children, we often believe we are not good enough to be loved. I had such a broken perception of my childhood and thought I was not worthy for most of my adult life. Every time my mother put herself first or didn't attend to my needs as a child, my story of not being loved grew. I know now as an adult; I was loved, and I am deeply worthy. Yet there are always versions of us that live on and react to this version of self-worth. To receive everything and more from this beautiful life, we truly need an inner story that reflects self-worth. Every time a decision within our life goes the wrong way, do you throw your hands in the air and say this is all too hard? When your boss gives you feedback, do you go home and sulk to your partner? These are all versions of your inner child at play, acting out from the past.

Affirmations have been around for thousands of years and are a large part of most spiritual practices within India too. There is also an ancient language called *Sanskrit* that is over 5000 years old. This ancient language holds very pure intention. A large part of yoga practices teaches affirmations within their dialogue and incorporate mantra. A mantra works similar to an affirmation, the subtle difference is how they're used, an affirmation is motivational whereas a mantra is held as sacred.

It's always about the balance of *intention* and *effort*: if your intention is to better yourself, with effort you shall receive. That's the secret behind every successful person in the world, your intentions and efforts bring forth a state of equilibrium giving balance to every aspect of your life. If your intention is coming from a place of love, you will never fail. Should your intention be based on making more money, well, you might have already failed. The intention of the affirmation we use is very important, that's why using ancient Sanskrit can be of benefit too.

These mantras have passed the test of time and have been passed down from guru to guru. One of my favourites is, "I am that I am." The yogic mantra "so hum" carries a contemplative meaning of "I am that" (so = "I am" and hum = "that"). Here, "that" refers to *all of creation*, the one breathing us all. For me, when I use this mantra, I feel content within the moment. It gives me a sense of knowing that who I am as a man, right now, however that may be, is more than okay. That whatever I've done or achieved is enough and 'I am that I am' is a deep level of self-acceptance. To go beyond that, it is all so a deep connection to all that is and all that will be. As men, we can be hard on ourselves, thinking we need to achieve great feats in life to be accepted and loved. If we break it down and reflect on the mantra, we witness something deep within ourselves. We observe we are a collection of our behaviours, from our parents and our past environment. Once we go beyond our patterns of what we are not, we can connect back to our true state.

As you can see, mantras and affirmations are powerful and have been around since the dawn of time. I suggest that you pull out your notebook and pen and sit them by your bedside table. I complete my affirmations every morning and night without fail. My other personal favourite is I meditate for twenty minutes morning and night. You can see that we are already starting to create a new story that will assist you in healing.

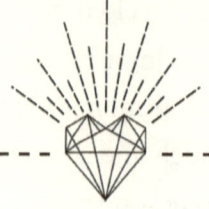

ACTIVITY: AFFIRMATIONS

A good brain hack is to use these *affirmations*, daily:

"I AM THAT I AM."

"I AM WORTHY."

This will help you change your mindset and cellular memory. Often our mind and deep self-worth is negative, by using this affirmation throughout our day it will help you slowly override your past and keep you anchored in the moment!

As we use the affirmation I am that I am, we have a more profound knowledge of who we are. We come to accept the parts of us that need the most love. Acceptance of who we are and where we have come from is one of life's true freedoms.

chapter four
fight-or-flight

I once undertook a leadership course at Roy Hill run by mining magnate Gina Rinehart, named as the world's richest woman. Roy Hill is a modern mining company, and my employer at the time, that introduced me to how the amygdala worked and broke down the flight or fight response. It was a turning point within my life and ultimately, the starting point of a two-year journey that would see me leave the business. To every member of Roy Hill who helped facilitate that course, thank you. Also, big thank you to Barry (CEO) for paying the bill. I would also like to thank a few key mentors that helped me in that adjustment period. The irony of a business educating their employees about the human body to a point they want to leave. You see, I learnt the paycheck I was receiving was not worth the stress and demand of my exhausted mind and body. My time at Roy Hill and the experiences and relationships formed were and still are priceless to me.

I would highly recommend Roy Hill as a place to be employed, especially the technology department if it is in alignment with your values. I'll now breakdown what I learnt and give you the simple version of a human fight-or-flight response.

An environmental input triggers a reaction within our mind and body. Say a heated conversation with our partner. Our natural intelligence then adjusts the chemicals within our mind and body to protect us from harm. This response is to apply resources to the correct parts of the body efficiently. The only problem is that this system is extremely outdated and is not keeping up with the modern world. That's why when you feel rage, you can witness an elevated heart rate and may not be thinking really clear. Our body prepares the mind, and the body, for battle. In the modern world, we can perceive conversations with our loved ones as a threat. There may be specific conversations or topics that seem threatening to us and stimulate our fight-or-flight response. And if we are suffering from PTSD, it can suspend us in a heightened state of reaction. We base this tendency to react on our military carriers and the conditioning we have received. I've also observed many people in the modern world who are so stimulated they find just about every conversation can trigger a fight-or-flight response within.

There are well over seven billion people in the world that potentially are relating to one another in a very unhealthy way. To compound this issue, our minds are aware of past threats and can pre-stimulate our fight-or-flight response before a trigger has even happened. Just the very risk of danger can be enough to cause us to stimulate. For example, if we think we saw a snake in the garden, we can get quite a significant response. Yet there was no snake, just the perception of a snake. So that difficult topic of conversation that may cause us to trigger with our partner could be viewed in a different light. Perhaps she was very reasonable in her request, yet in the past it was a difficult situation. An experience that we may hold on to could influence our present moment and our ability to respond. This is a great example of the human mind protecting itself by taking past experiences and then applying them to future events. It's perception!

We then have the tendency to apply past difficult situations to new situations and recreate the pain all over again. We have become experts at using past difficult situations to project our current circumstances. A touchy subject is only touchy because perhaps we are still offended by a memory or an event in the past that's relatable to the current touchy subject today. Often a large portion of these past situations can be related to our childhood and shape our very identity. Our hobbies, romantic interests, work choices are all based on a previous experience that's projected into the future. I often wonder how much of this fight or-flight life response that exists are because of our connection to war. I believe that western society has created a modern-day world where we are constantly feeling threatened. Continually working to fuel out-of-control spending habits and materialistic approaches towards life. With a gym and cafe on every corner, we as a species are needing unprecedented levels of stimulation just to function.

So how do we change this? By becoming aware. The more aware you become, the more you will deeply understand what is controlling a large portion of your ability to relate. When we are connecting with such a flawed mechanism, it's within our best interest to understand it in depth. Try to develop a new level of awareness, even bring up a conversation with someone that has a history of being difficult, with the 'right' intention to change the story you perceive. Observe the other person and also witness yourself, place your awareness in your body and note what arises. Should you struggle to achieve this, first, try following your breath to help you bring an awareness into your body. By simply becoming more aware in the moment we are taking greater responsibility and creating a better growth mindset.

Let's look at the fight-or-flight responses from the perspective of a soldier. A soldier's workload and training are designed to stimulate a fight-or-flight response. It is under this duress that we learn to make quick decisions. In this state of fight-or-flight, our system is injecting our body with cortisol and adrenaline. Through a combination of nerve and hormonal signals, your adrenal glands release the surge of adrenaline and cortisol. Adrenaline increases your heart rate, elevates your blood pressure and boosts energy supplies. That is why over time these hormones can become addictive to our body.

Once we encounter our first traumatic event, the mind is on alert, ready to be extra diligent. Our mind may project past situations to the future looking to create a story, so it can protect us. It's a beautiful process and something we have unconsciously been repeating since childhood. On the downside, the mind can perceive any situation to be dangerous with minimal evidence. If we have already become addicted to the dangerous levels of adrenaline and cortisol in the body, this is a problem. We are already out of alignment and will struggle to process or move past the incident. Instead, the mind will become fixated and use this to refuel our addiction.

As the basis of our training and working conditions are based on fear this can have a very stimulating effect. This stimulation can still be present even when the threat is not. Our mind is always going to weigh the evidence in our favour of stress to continue the cycle. This is factual that our perception of a past memory will be swayed to make us feel correct or safe. So, as we store memories of the past, they aren't factual to the actual events. Now we can see basing our future interactions on possibly incorrect data. Yes, that's correct, the perceived threat or situation does not even need to be real.

Once our environment stimulates our fight-or-flight response it is hard to break the cycle. Even if the stimulation was removed our mind could still keep us in this heightened state of alert. With a large amount of our disconnection formed within the military, it's difficult to reconnect and stop this cycle of stimulation. This state feels healthy or normal and acceptable.

Another coping mechanism we're privy to is using substances such as alcohol and drugs, which further disconnects us from our emotions and switches off the stimulation. I don't think most of us even know what we are trying to escape from at the time, it's a pattern we're not even conscious of. This behaviour may have developed in childhood, so embedded within we don't even notice it. When I'd return from deployment I'd be hyper-vigilant for some time. Taking the past tempo of the deployment and applying it to home life. Often drinking excessively to the point of a blackout or not being able to recall the evening. It would be pretty obvious when your partner calls you out on these unconscious behaviours. Once we take the time to reflect and look around, we see our behaviour is irrational. Yet, often as soldiers, we label our excessive drinking and disconnection methods as the body's inability to process trauma.

Once we have a large amount of stimulation within our system, it has more than likely caused multiple incomplete fight-or-flight responses. These responses are activated but never fully witnessed or removed from the body. That's why we are still holding on to these past experiences because we have not honoured our body's natural process. However, there is a way to complete this natural response. In later topics, I'll discuss how breathwork can help us remove our incomplete fight-or-flight responses. This can have a tremendous amount of release and assist our body and mind to recalibrate itself. For any soldier who has ever faced battle, we are still holding on to this tension. Often these experiences and fight-or-flight responses can remain within the body for years and years.

The stress and level of damage that these processes can leave is remarkable. Until resolved this level of stress can cause havoc to our overall health and wellbeing. As we still hold on our minds are still scanning for a similar threat to relate to. As we continually scan for a similar threat, this becomes very taxing on our body. We're always in a state of recreating a story over and over just so we can protect ourselves. For soldiers who have suffered traumatic events, protecting ourselves is no different. These complex traumas live on inside our body and shape the people we are today. With traditional therapy, this deeply embedded trauma may still be residual in the body. Our nervous system is still holding on like a giant spring that has been compressed and needs to be released.

By using the power of the breath in later chapters, we understand how we can remove this trauma from the body, nervous system and from the mind. I have seen remarkable changes in my personality and even my body shape and size from using breathwork.

BREATHWORK IS A POTENT HEALING MODALITY.

Bringing more awareness to our fight and flight response will allow us to move forward in our lives. With intention and effort, we have an endless potential for change. Regardless of your personal circumstances, you can make a conscious choice for change. It is perfectly normal to have these reactions within the body or create stories from past stimulation in our minds.

Yet we must take responsibility now. By turning our awareness inward and understanding who we are as males and witnessing our behaviour we will significantly change. When we reflect on our behaviour, patterns, speech and thoughts, we become more aware of the effect the outside world is having on us within. After observing our reactions, we realise the importance of the ability to *respond* not *react*. With every healthy choice, our ability to respond grows stronger.

By changing our perception of the outside world through our awareness, we can limit the amount we react. We can observe more of the outside world and our own internal world. We do not have to judge what we are witnessing but just observe. Changing our perception of the past can be very profound. If we look back with greater acceptance, this limits how we react or trigger. Understanding who we are and where we have come from are a large part of the healing process. As we accept the past, it should not limit our desire to change and move forward. We are just maintaining a positive perception of our reality in the past to limit the triggers in our current moment.

Change of perception has been a game changer for me to and has immensely dissolved my triggers and negative reactions. I now believe that everything can be viewed with a neutral mindset and this greatly assisted healing my heart. By not seeing the world as one continuous threat, I took back control of my world. In my perception upgrade, I found stillness and unpacked the past and what I was holding on to. I wholly believe that my daily meditation practice greatly assisted my process. I began with as little as five minutes to centre myself and built my meditation up to twenty minutes every morning. To be honest, I am meditating beyond that now, but twenty minutes is a great place to start. When we have greater control of our minds, we can influence our thoughts, actions and behaviours. It's through our increased cognitive function that we change our perception of our reality.

When I finally was ready to look inward, I could see that my nervous system was crying out for help. Meditation relaxed me to a point where I could switch off the stimulation in my body. I believe I was in a heightened state of living for close to fifteen years. It was not until I improved my diet and started a regular meditation practice that I pressed the pause button on my old life and way of being. My sleep immensely improved, and my body could finally rest in its natural calm state. When this massive change happened, I also developed symptoms of adrenal fatigue, another blessing to listen to my body and receive this deep rest. This was a period I honoured and still am. I take a rest when I need to, and I've removed any workouts I was doing and honoured this new message from my body. This is an example of changing your perception. Just because my energy can be low, I still see this as a gift. This change has been my body responding to the change.

If you have any symptoms of adrenal fatigue such as sleepy eyes in the morning, lack of energy and extreme mood swings, seek help. Sadly, out of two veteran friendly doctors, not one of them was on the ball with a treatment plan. I would highly recommend a naturopath to start a holistic approach. I have no doubt through a combination of healthy eating, meditation, breathwork and sleep hygiene we can heal our physical body from the years of abuse.

I had my CAR (Cortisol Awaking Response) tested. This is the pre-cursor to adrenaline and cortisol and was tested six times throughout the course of a day. The results showed that when I woke up in the morning, my cortisol was off the charts and would fall by the day's end to allow me to sleep. If we have accelerated rates of cortisol and adrenaline in the body, our fight-or-flight response can be extreme and very unpleasant. A naturopath or functional medicine doctor can test your levels. Many natural supplements exist to lower our levels. Combing these supplements with limited phone time at night and candlelight after dark is a great place to start. Consume good fats in your diet and stay away from any sugar that will spike your energy and cause a crash. By treating our adrenal glands, we can lower our reactions. I have had very extreme and over the top reactions that can last for thirty minutes to an hour. My symptoms would include everything from screaming, violence, road rage and more. We are not broken and we sure as hell don't need to be doped up on drugs to fix these episodes. The body has the natural ability to heal with time. When we fill it with healthy food and a nourishing environment, the damage that has been done while in service can be corrected.

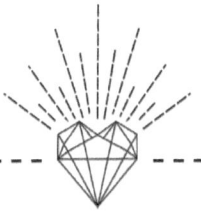

ACTIVITY: VISUALISATION

Find a place where you feel safe, picture a location or situation that you know can cause you to trigger. This may be a supermarket or some other public place. Picture yourself totally owning that environment, confident deep belly breathing, a big smile and a strong sense of pride for your calmness in this situation.

The stronger you make the visualisation and the more positive the emotions you attach to it, the quicker you will change the story within your mind. As you do this visualisation, continue to breathe deep into your belly.

THE BREATHING IS YOUR ANCHOR.

When you are next in this environment, be sure to engage your breathing. This is your anchor that will bring you back to your positive visualisation and will help you feel safe and calm. Set an intention to remain calm and override your past nervous or feeling of not feeling safe.

chapter five
the present moment

Mediation is powerful!

You can download many meditation apps and find millions of free online guided and non-guided meditations. You may not see an improvement overnight, but make no mistake mediation will help you expand, level up and heal. Reducing stress and anxiety, allowing you increased cognitive function, hormone balancing, increased feelings of peace and control of suicidal thoughts, and many more benefits exist. I have just finished teaching a beginner's meditation course at the Pyramids of Chi in Ubud, Bali. What an amazing place to be a part of and expand my healing. I highly recommend this establishment. Magic happens there on the daily and the owners Peter and Lynn have genuinely put their entire life on hold to be of service.

I find the real magic happens when you open your eyes after a meditation. By applying a *new* cognitive function and awareness, you cultivate a *new* life. The magnificence is also when you apply the newfound skills in the real world. For example, as we meditate, we are becoming more of the observer as we simply witness of our thoughts without judgement. It's important not to become attached to your thoughts and also not to identify with them. So, when we open our eyes, we can apply the same principles.

WE CAN BECOME THE OBSERVER OF LIFE ITSELF.

A lot of our unhealthy masculine behaviours begin with a *thought* and that thought becomes a *feeling* and then thought and feeling become an *action*. In meditation we learn to observe any thoughts that rise and let them go by observing. The more we meditate, the more we increase the ability to be the observer. This is a very powerful step.

I had a very masculine and dark sense of humour from my time in the Army. I've found some of those traits are not in alignment with the new vision of me, some of them I have even found to be inappropriate. So, by meditating, I strengthened the gap between thoughts, the ability to respond *and* withhold any jokes that may not be appropriate. Some people think it's just their humour and be okay with telling unhealthy masculine jokes. But I hear you, brother, and I was once that guy. Not anymore. That me was just a product of yesterday, from my father and his father before that. Often our dark humour can be a coping mechanism to cope with the stress from our service. Our humour is not our own yet. It's something we have inherited from our environment. You are the person standing in this moment with the ability to be anyone. The person who can let go of his past can truly create any version of himself through meditation.

One reason meditation is so powerful is it helps us see the invisible. By the invisible I mean the unconscious behaviour that is so ingrained in us we don't even know it's there. There are types of meditation that can help you increase this specifically. By increasing our awareness, we can witness more of our own behaviour in each moment. This is a beautiful gift. We can observe the initial thought before we feel anxiety. Once we witness this initial thought and recognise the feeling within our body, we can sit with this feeling. Feel it, give it space and acceptance rather than judging it. We breathe and connect with our centred self and remove the thoughts and the emotion. We journal or communicate with our partners about how we are feeling. There are multiple options available, the main thing is we must connect to our inner world and not disconnect.

Observation meditation is another powerful meditation to train our mind to become a witness. We sit in a comfortable position, close our eyes, and watch our thoughts. I have labelled my thoughts as useful and not useful at the start of my meditation journey. The most important part is not participating in the thought. By that, I mean the mind has a natural tendency to group thoughts. Suddenly, you have a story you are participating in and have lost your concentration. So, by labelling our thoughts as not useful and then not participating, we are training our brain. We are strengthening the cognitive function that even if a negative thought arises, we can just observe them and let them pass. Once we open our eyes, we take this ability out into the world and can actively apply it to any moment. So, if you were to have a sudden thought of fear arise, we could label this as not useful.

Mastering this in life gives us a new ability to become a witness in any moment and any negative thought pattern, which is powerful. Once we remove the natural tendency of the mind to have negative thoughts, we can strengthen positive thoughts. We can do this by consciously reframing our perception of any given situation to be more positive and to be of assistance. By taking control and responsibility of our mind, we can create limitless potential. Our thoughts, our words and our actions are now supporting us to heal in every minute of every day for our entire life.

Recently I sought assistance from the Australian Government for free medical treatment for PTSD. In my dealing with the Department of Veterans' Affairs, I noticed the anger and rage that still existed in me around authority. Just from one email in my inbox, *bang,* I was met with internal anger and a large story that come flooding back to be witnessed. I thought, *Shit, this can't happen, I'm meant to be Zen level 1000.* I used my thought observation technique.

I also mentioned to my partner about still having such a problem with authority. Outbursts of anger are perfectly normal for someone that has suffered from trauma. Especially if you are now open and giving yourself extra permission to feel this anger. I have given myself full permission to feel and let all my anger out. Yet what I did next was take responsibility for my actions. I meditated on the Army and my father and removed the negative attachment towards authority.

On that same day I went out to a small forest in the hills of Perth and did some yelling therapy. There were parts of me that were still extremely angry inside me that needed to be released. When I think about it deeply my body must have been deeply angry with how it was treated. Working for multiple days without food or sleep. Training for multiple weeks with a broken foot. Eating the same toxic food for weeks on end. Listening to old stubborn warrant officers yell for no reason. Daily rocket attacks for months and exposure to digital graphic material such as drone footage and beheadings. For ten years I had gone against every natural feeling within my body. No wonder I was angry. No wonder my system needed to rebalance itself.

If you have not tried yelling out in the wilderness if you are angry, I highly recommend this. After this amazing release, I then created a new story for myself that I happily accepted authority in my life. It truly can be that simple. Through meditation we create stillness and can identify with the cause of our anger. Once we have found the cause, we do the work to release it. There is no magic pill or doctors visit to undo the years of neglect we put our body and minds through in service. We heal ourselves by taking responsibility for our emotions that arise to be witnessed and then go inward. We do this by putting in effort. The more we put in, the more we receive.

Another favourite meditation that I find really helps me is mantra based. This can be explained quickly as just meditating with a few simple words repeated in your mind. The words are positive, and we can use any language. The words act as an anchor for your mind and can greatly assist you drifting off to deep states of stillness. Through this mediation we increase our ability to strengthen our cognitive function, to stay in the present moment.

THE TRUE MAGIC OF LIFE IS ONLY EVER FOUND IN THE PRESENT MOMENT.

This is how we tap into our power. By training our minds through a mantra-based mediation to stay in the present moment. Once again, when we open our eyes, that's where the fun begins. Too often is our mind trying to take us to the past or to the future. As we drift towards the future and create multiple possibility's that don't exist, we let go of the magic in the present moment. If we are creating stories of us having PTSD and identifying with the past, we are automatically placing our mind in a story. This is attaching the past to our current present moment and blocking any chance we have at truly at enjoying what is present in the now. So, we can use a mantra-based mediation when our eyes are open. There are multiple teachings from all around the world that suggest repeating a mantra every day.

If we feel our mind is recalling the past, we can use the mantra in that present moment. As we drift to the past and attach to our thoughts, we know that it will snowball and turn into a feeling. So, by repeating the mantra, we bring ourselves back to the present moment. We also strengthen our mind's ability not to wander to the past or future and remain more present in life. To have the ability to remain in the present moment is the key to a happy and amazing life. As you can tell, meditation can have a profound effect on our natural negative responses. We were born in the present moment and that freedom we once had as children to truly witness and enjoy life is achievable as an adult if we approach every moment with a childlike curiosity. The trick is to stop limiting the present moment to unfold how we would expect it to. By staying open to what potentially could happen is a magical skill in itself.

I suggest an app called Insight Timer. This app has millions of the best meditation teachers from across the globe offering free mediations, and I would highly recommend teacher Davidji as a great place to start. I have uploaded free mediations that have been recorded to assist not just soldiers but all people that are suffering from trauma. Whatever mediation your heart desires can be found on this app. It also has the unique ability to make friends with other meditators in your local area. This is a pretty cool feature and a way to possibly meet like-minded friends.

My daily routine around meditation can vary depending on how I am feeling. Every day, as soon as the light hits my eyes, I run through what I'm grateful for. This can be a pretty long list: happy to be alive, happy to breathe, happy for a great night's sleep and so on. These positive thought patterns go a long way to retrain your brain to stay in a positive and gratitude mindset. I also build a visualisation of the future me, happy and whole. I visualise my goals to help create a better world. Then I mediate for at least twenty minutes. By introducing simple breathing exercises in or after your mediation, you supercharge your day. When we create this level of stillness in the morning, we can then carry that state of peace and calm into our daily lives. Whatever life throws at us after that, we have a good platform to respond and not react.

If we think about our time in the military, we often would set multiple alarms before we went to sleep, fearful of not being late to work. For ten years, every day, I was in a place of fear and over-stimulation before I slept. Then I'd wake up to an alarm and get ready at the speed of light to get off to work. One of my most favourite things to do these days is have the most relaxing morning ever. I won't even take my phone off flight mode for at least two hours after waking up. As mentioned, I had a job after the Army that did not allow me to live this lifestyle. So, I traded my paycheck for peace and stillness and healing. This stillness and relaxation have allowed my body the time to relax and heal. We can all make choices to heal. All you have to do is open your mind to new possibilities. We can create stillness in chaos.

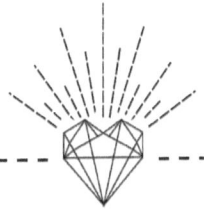

ACTIVITY: BREATHING TECHNIQUE

The present moment is powerful, and it is everywhere we go. We often relate our interpretation of the present moment to our pattern of breathing. Even if our environment is safe, but our breathing is shallow, our mind can interpret that as a threat and be on high alert.

Take a few moments to become aware of your breath while reading this. Is your breath deep? Is it shallow? Are your ribs stuck? Is it not present within your belly? Try it throughout your day! The deeper we breathe, the more we are healing our body in every moment.
Try taking thirty deep breaths and imagine breathing down into your hips.

chapter six
emotional stress

As males we have become experts at disconnecting from our emotions. Every time we get angry or disconnected, we're not connecting and honouring how we are *truly* feeling within. If we are constantly at the gym, often this is just a disguised coping mechanism for a stressful life. Drinking alcohol and drug use is also another coping mechanism for dealing with emotional stress. A good way to gauge the amount of stress you're under is to witness your language. If you find you are more negative when you communicate to the outside world, this may be an indicator of how negative your inside world is. If you are quick to judge and blame others, you may be judging and blaming yourself your actions or for your unhappiness.

There has also been a stigma around women not knowing men *do* have emotions. The truth is, men are not cold and closed off. On the surface, this may appear true, yet every man wants to emotionally express themselves, they just don't know how. They don't know how to connect with emotions that may have been suppressed for generations. The opposite is true. Once we understand our capacity and ability to feel and express our emotions, we stop bottling things up. This connection is critical to heal from our past trauma. Our lineage of war has suppressed our emotions, we know this. And when it gets too tough, we shut down only as a protection mechanism and often don't know how to open up again. The state comes in many forms: from telling a bad joke, drinking and taking drugs, or ending a relationship. Emotional stress is real for men and is common in today's society.

You can see just within the Australian Defence Force there have been 138 suicides in 2017 and 2018. This number is very alarming. It shows not only are males disconnecting from emotions; they are disconnected from the ability to ask for help or receive it. I want to let all my brothers out there know there is always help. You are worthy to receive help, and you are worthy to ask for help. Many times, on this path, I have reached out to a general practitioner, leading functional doctors within Perth, only to be turned away. That's true, these leading doctors in holistic health said they could *not* help a soldier with PTSD. At first, this made me furious, and I felt defeated, as though no one out there gave a shit and I thought, *What's the point?* Emotional stress is real, and we must understand the impact that this is having on us. As we trigger emotional stressors, we are activating our fight-or-flight response, and this has consequences.

The consequences of fight-or-flight response are toxic. It's even been said that cortisol affects the hippocampus, which is the part of the brain that judges and assesses our level of stress. We recognise uncontrollable stress influences the hippocampus at various levels of analysis. Behaviourally, human studies have found that stress generally impairs various hippocampal-dependent memory tasks. So yes, our service in the military affects us long after we leave.

There have been four types of stress classified with the first one "being emotional". I know first-hand what it is like to be away ten months of the year and what that did to my partner and my personal health. The fracture this causes in families in relationships is the very definition of emotional stress. As soldiers, we're training hard and being subjected to stress at work. Upon that are other stressors like trying to empathise with a partner and loved one back home as we try to understand what they are going through. Layering on this, when we are deployed overseas to foreign environments our body undergoes more stress. The fear of the unknown and the stress of leaving our partners at home are natural human reactions. We know a certain level of stress is by design and part of our training to make us ready for battle, yet the real battle is with our health and wellbeing. Our mental and emotional states are closed and dissociated. With pre-deployment training and time overseas, we can be overstimulated for a whole year or more. And when our neurotransmitters become frayed, it's a case of robbing Peter to pay Paul. We work and live in a system that is purposely designed to lower our personal state of mental health and wellness. This only makes us true masters of overstimulation, unhealthy men that go against our natural design.

TO HEAL, WE NEED TO FEEL.

We are not here to solve our problems of the past yet to feel them, and in this, they dissolve. One key to breaking the patterns of the past is to understand what our current hormone and neurotransmitters are doing. Functional doctors are leading the way in analysing what effects stress is having on our body. You can undergo an awaking cortisol response saliva test to see where your levels are at. I'll talk more about this later.

Now, I'll introduce you to a concept called 'emotional addiction'. This is where the brain is subconsciously scanning the environment for the emotion we are addicted to. This could be the emotion that raises our cortisol and adrenaline. It's as though the brain always on alert to find something that piques that rise in cortisol and adrenaline. Yes, our brain is like an addict scanning television shows, eves dropping on conversations, reading social media posts for this emotional HIT. This is often what we might refer to as a trigger, something external that triggers our internal emotions. Once we receive this emotion—let's use stress for example—our brain and our nervous system responds to the perceived environment. You become elated, familiar with the high, and then you come crashing down to only seek that feeling again and again. These cycles of behaviour are real and, most importantly, they do not define us.

Often these cycles are a by-product of our service and our genetic relationship with stress. In these cycles, our behaviour may become questionable. We can break these cycles. Our family history often defines our genetic predisposition. Perhaps you had a tough upbringing and saw trauma before the military. I promise you, any form of bad behaviour you are experiencing within PTSD can be witnessed and moved through so you can be a better version of yourself. Through awareness and hard work we can break any emotional addiction and correct the natural balance within our brain.

**ONCE WE FIND PEACE WITHIN,
WE FIND PEACE AGAIN IN THE OUTSIDE WORLD.**

chapter seven
physical stress

The amount of excessive exercise we endured in the military may also have contributed to the imbalances we are coping with now. We know emotional and physical stressors are injecting us with unhealthy levels of hormones. Studies have shown serious adrenal issues with members in CrossFit gyms being tested just a few weeks after starting. There are positive mental aspects of training, yet they become counterproductive when the training levels become more of an addiction. On entering basic training, I fractured a bone in my foot with about three weeks to go. They'd branded the rehabilitation platoon with shame and negativity since day one, and I did not see this as an option. So, I took around ten ibuprofen a day and soldiered on. In our field phase, I would make sure I was up earlier to eat some food and then take my pills. On some days, I couldn't and would consume the pills on an empty stomach. Not my best move. I'm well aware of the real dangers associated with this choice, yet I was determined to march on.

My CPL and section leader saw and understood what I was doing to march on. They did not condone my behaviour. They considered it *my* choice. On marching into my new next training unit, I couldn't train for twelve months as I needed medical treatment to fix my foot that had deteriorated. I was non-weight bearing for four months, then had my foot placed in plaster and then conducted a five-month rehabilitation cycle. This is where my real addiction with exercise was ignited.

As we've learnt, we can become addicted to emotions, we can also become addicted to exercise. I remember my ex-partner telling me, 'You're addicted to exercise?' I disagreed, thinking I just liked to train. And just like every addict, I couldn't see my problem. Turns out she was right, and the constant training soon lead to injury and my inability to cope with my emotional stress. Physical stress is real. You can see a similar pattern in elite sports players who leave the game and abuse alcohol and drugs. They have similar symptoms to PTSD, they have suffered from emotional, physical and environmental stress. Their body is so addicted to emotions running through their blood that they too look for different coping mechanisms. There are thousands of examples of elite sportspersons trying to cope with vast amounts of emotional and physical addiction. Many people may argue otherwise, that this is just a choice and the path they have chosen.

When we break down what drives a man, we can see it's his thoughts triggering his emotions and together they both make his actions. So, if the brain is continually scanning for a particular rush or emotion, his thoughts and emotions will in doubt create his actions. Once we realise what is driving us, we can take control of our thoughts to break this pattern. By setting an intention to heal, we can work towards changing our thoughts. Once we understand that our behaviour can be assisted physically, through diet we can really change the game. With the assistance of hormone balancing substances, we are well on the path to stabilising our thoughts, emotions and actions. Make no mistake with the correct help you can correct the deepest of trauma, there is always help. Ensure your intention is to heal, speak it aloud, write it down and use your actions to align with your intention.

WITH PURE INTENTION AND EFFORT, YOU CAN'T FAIL.

chapter eight
environmental stress

As soldiers, we have all seen the negativity that exists within our troops. The stress or the frustration that we have directed to the headquarters. This is happening for two reasons. The first one is that we have an emotional addiction to feeling stressed. Second is our body and our natural intelligence can associate that work and the officers are the most likely cause. The officers are also just stuck in a loop, completing what is expected of them by the system. Guess what one of the easiest ways to keep a person in a heightened state is? Lack of information. In this day and age, we have extreme amounts of digital information at our fingertips. Besides the lottery numbers, there is not much information in the world that we can't find through our smartphone.

So how do you think the modern-day soldier's mind is coping when he's at work and has no idea what he could be doing five minutes from now? He experiences feelings of anxiousness and fear. The fear of the unknown is a large environmental stressor and is having large effects on our internal stimulation. Often when it was time to post across the other side of the country, you would not know the location of your new house. This in terms would limit your partner's ability to find a job. They weave this level of uncertainty through everyday life within the military. This is helping us respond at a moment's notice to the unknown. Did I elected to be a soldier as a young man? Yes. Was I aware of the physical effects that this would have on me during and after my service? No.

Was the military sustainable in the early days with the limited amount of environmental stimulation after work? Has the rest of the world and the stimulation increased? Is the modern Army and the outside stimulation creating some new form of mental health tipping point? One problem with the modern world and the environment we live in, it's hard to escape. We are looking at our phones before we go to sleep and as soon as we wake up. The world is right in our face and so is our ability to find the stress or the emotion we are looking for all too easy. Many soldiers around the globe find surfing is greatly assisting their PTSD. Surfing is a great way to be involved with nature. Surfing is a form of a moving meditation, and it's beautiful to witness the amazing effects these programs have on soldiers. By changing our environment, we have a great ability to heal.

I am always amazed at the coping mechanisms of the human body. While deployed to Afghanistan and operating out of Kandahar Airfield, I was subjected to around 50-100 rocket attacks. This is an example of environmental stress, a good example at that. To be honest, you lose count and your care factor becomes minimal to the fact your life is in danger. Lucky for me, the Taliban weren't all that great at aiming their rockets towards our base. Other soldiers were not lucky, and attacks even penetrated the Australian bombproof accommodation. Should a rocket attack be heard, our directive was to get on the floor, then head to a bombproof shelter. After a while, we noticed one of our det members was having a healthy human reaction to getting attacked. He would appear nervous and be quick to get on the ground. The rest of us would jump on his back like a form of dark humour to cope with the near possible death experience. We made light of these dark situations to cope with our environmental stressors.

I was working in a stimulating environment and my emotional addiction "stress" was way too easy to find in this role. It wasn't until I truly stepped back from work that I could realise the extent of my past behaviours and patterns playing out within me. I was still so stimulated that I was getting angry every day at work. Then using multiple coping mechanisms to disconnect from the amount of stress I was creating. I take full responsibility that I was in a loop and acting like a goose to my fellow co-workers and employees.

Yeah, my bad.

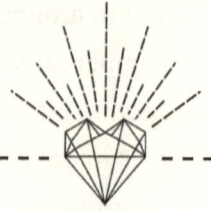

ACTIVITY: OBSERVATION

Take a moment to witness the environmental stress that exists in your life.

Make a mental note of all the things you find difficult to deal with or you find stressful.

Now, take a moment to trace the source of that stress. Is it your perception? Your interpretation? Or are you just straight up creating this stress in your life from your own bullshit stories?

chapter nine
nutritional stress

As soldiers, we know in our time of need we had limited access to nutritional food. In times of need, I mean at war, forward operating bases or on exercise. Our bodies and minds are being subjected to large amounts of stress that could continue for days. I have been involved in multiple exercises and deployments where we were expected to carry a live weapon with no sleep. To add to these harsh environmental conditions, they gave us rations filled with sugar, preservatives and artificial colouring. We were being exposed to high amounts of environmental stress. We are also being exposed to nutritional stress. The body's natural ability to deal with stress and trauma is deeply related to how our body functions and the fuel we provide it. How could we ever expect our body or mind to process environmental stress when we were living off a highly processed diet?

For years in the Army, they taught us the same lessons over and over. For anyone that has served in the Australian Army, the annually played heat video was always a source of stress. Not one of these annual lessons assisted to minimise the possible effects of our stressful environment. No mention of how we as soldiers could limit the workplace stress through choices of our own.

There is a certain level of neglect in the level of education that the Army is giving its modern-day soldiers. Yes, we understand that in war and exercises nutrition can't be further explored. Yet basic education and basic awareness on mental health and early indicators to PTSD would go a long way to raising awareness. To change the relationship that many soldiers have with the concept of having PTSD. Meditation is not a food but nourishing to the mind and body. Through education and simple practices, we can assist soldiers adapt to the environmental stress they are experiencing as opposed to suppressing it. Many soldiers within the Australian Army would attend morning PT without eating breakfast or without consuming any healthy fats. When people are suffering from adrenal fatigue, this pattern can be very destructive. Having healthy fats in the morning has greatly assisted in my recovery from adrenal fatigue. Every time our body is burning high fructose or no food such as fasting, this is placing additional stress on our already overused adrenal glands. Basic education like this could help soldiers change some small behaviours to greatly assist their body in the long run.

Depending on the length of your service and the intensity, your body's ability to even absorb nutrition can be greatly affected.

Trauma affects our liver, stomach and physical body and the way it can be stored and manifest itself in the body. You can consult naturopaths on ways for you to explore how you could be under nutritional stress because of your physical stress. I have completely changed my diet and am undergoing treatment for my gut by taking natural herbs and colonics to undo the years of damage that I have experienced. Often whilst under constant fight-or-flight responses, our bowels can be affected and stop some nutritional absorptions. Yet stored trauma and emotions in the body can keep our bodies trapped in a certain state, regardless of the food consumed. We must shift the trapped and stored energy along with nutritional support. I don't want to go too much into detail as I am not a specialist. However, I highly recommend that you speak with a functional medicine doctor or naturopath and express with them any of your symptoms that you may be experiencing.

Often our high stress environment within and after our service life can leave us eating our meals at the speed of light. This is truly a reflection of our nervous system and our relationship with food. By eating quickly often we are not in a parasympathetic state, responsible for our food digestions. This can then limit our body's ability to absorb our food and even process. As often eating our food at the speed light we are also not chewing our food and making it more difficult for you to digest and break down. Most of all, we are not taking the time to appreciate how blessed we are to receive the amazing food available in the world at the moment. As we become more aware around our eating habits and slow down, we can truly create new beliefs within our body that it's safe to stop and eat and enjoy our food.

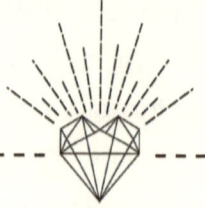

ACTIVITY: SET AN INTENTION

Set the intention to create a new behaviour at mealtimes. Express this to your partner or friends if it may help you. Picture yourself at the next mealtime, slowing down and taking the time to chew your food. Savour the food and give yourself space between mouthfuls. At first, I would recommend doing this in silence as it will help you stay focused and change your relationship with food. It's also going to activate your parasympathetic nervous system to help you digest and get the maximum nutritional benefits from our food.

chapter ten
yoga

In this part of the book, I'm going to introduce you to the modalities I discovered that supported my healing.

When I was in my healing process, I didn't have a daily yoga practice, although I dabbled when my body felt the call. The state of my adrenals also benefited from a Yin yoga style whilst healing. The gentleness and structure of Yin yoga can greatly assist healing the body. Yin yoga is available to everyone via multiple free phone apps. We live in times where our location and resources do not restrict our ability to heal. Yin yoga allows you to be gentle on your body and not expend too much energy in any given class. It can feel like a two-hour moving meditation whilst holding deep restorative poses. The focus of Yin yoga is to stay connected to your breath with your eyes closed or downcast. The gentle movement can remove some damage we've done to our nervous system and body.

After my time from serving in the Army, I had damaged parts of my body with major injury to my right knee, shoulder and lower back. So, creating the flexibility needed to reach certain holds in Yin can be challenging, especially if you've had an injury. Yet in this difficulty, we can release deep tension within our body that has lived with us for many years. Typically, a class will have one instructor who guides you through a series of longer poses held up to seven minutes. It's a safe and relaxed environment. In these classes we really have a heightened ability to feel into our body. We reconnect with our body and listen to the messages it's showing us. There was a certain level of trust and reconnection that I found.

For many years I would participate in double workouts five to six days a week in CrossFit and other body breaking workouts. Often, I was pushing through the natural messages when my body was telling me to *stop*. We must master our minds in our service to push past the barriers with our mind. Yet as this continues for years and years, there is an extreme level of disconnection that is caused within. In Yin yoga there is no escaping the communication with your body and you can reconnect to listen in silence and be gentle with yourself. Seven minutes of hip opening is work within itself, so the typical male approach must be amended and met with grace and ease. In this gentleness, you will not only feel amazing after leaving the class, your body, posture and flexibility will match your new emotional state. I have directly experienced many profound healing and emotional shifts in yoga. Yoga still follows the same principles of all healing modalities, intention and effort. I recommend that you include Yin yoga in your healing because as we shift the attachment of yesterday, we really need to take a body, mind and soul approach.

AS WE CLAIM MORE SPACE IN OUR BODY, WE LET GO OF PAST ATTACHMENT.

chapter eleven
nourishment and self-love

The better our diet, the better we feel, think and perform. We can't heal from trauma should we still consume the wrong foods. If we consciously eat the wrong foods, we can't feel the power that exist within the present moment. This does not mean that you need to make drastic changes overnight, but each food choice should be a healthy one. Good foods give us the essential energy to make healthy choices. When you think about it, how could anyone who has a bad diet ever make the healthy choices when they are not fuelling themselves correctly? By eating more fresh fruit and vegetables and limiting preservatives and gluten, we can dramatically change our relationship with food.

Food is another relationship we have with our body and mind, the more effort and awareness we place towards food, the more we can get from it. Taking responsibility for our food choices is a great way to show up in other areas in our life. Normally, from a male's perspective, we would eat to fill our bodies or satisfy a gym routine. It is possible to change our perspective to see food as something that can heal our trauma. Our relationship with food is so profound we must take the time to understand what is driving our food choices.

Ask yourself why you feel compelled to eat ice-cream after dinner. This food choice could show us that we are lacking something or perhaps addicted to something, like sugar or adrenaline. Food choices are a great way to see if we are eating from a place of *emotion* rather than *nourishment*. Food is a key element for us to take more responsibility for our minds. So, if you are drinking alcohol or taking drugs, you must reduce this to a level where you can feel good and make healthy choices.

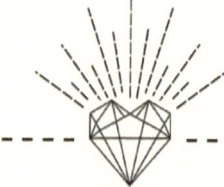

**ACTIVITY:
FUTURE YOU VISUALISATION**

I've found building a vision really helps with me to correct habits or behaviours.
Take a moment to close your eyes and envision a version of you in the future of full health. You could envision more colour in your face, an improved posture or weight loss.

> Now, in that moment, envision you have eaten and made healthy choices. Now, we fill in the blanks to achieve that vision.
>
> This is what I call intention and effort.
>
> Every healing modality in the world works this way.
>
> The visualisation here is the intention and part of the effort. The more frequently we build this visualisation, the easier it will be for you to change from your old patterns.

The real effort comes after you have opened your eyes. Making poor food choices can also come from a place of low self-worth, not thinking we are worthy of a great life and healthy body.

My self-worth is increasing every day, and so are my food choices. It's been a slow progression, but I had an extremely poor diet for the first twenty-five years of my life. I would overeat as a child and as a young adult to compensate for my low self-worth. I would choose comfort food to detach from the emotions I was feeling, or more importantly, *not* feeling.

For years, if I was stressed, overworked, or not feeling loved, I would reach for something to escape this sensation. That could be anything from over-exercising, alcohol, drugs, sex, or a sugar hit, like ice-cream. At the time, I was extremely unaware of these choices. These substances would create a place within me where I felt comfortable, loved or even happy. Yet ultimately, they were just distracting me from the pain in my heart or the past. I had a very limited ability to understand my emotions at the time.

My emotions were also compounding the problem. So how do we change this? Meditation and affirmations were integral in my first steps of changing my diet. I would wake up every morning and write on a piece of paper what I wanted to change. I'd repeat the process at night. I would hold the vision of me feeling healthy and healed.

To even start writing this book I walked around saying, 'I'm an avid writer.' It can be that simple by creating a new story we can reprogram our minds to work with us and not against us. I even used the same process to quit cigarettes. It was easy. I completed the above and then a few days later my craving subsided and a new version of me began. Through visualisation techniques, the mind believes our new reality and our body comes along for the ride. If the option to smoke a cigarette was to arise, the mind would look at the story we have created and know that's not in alignment with our intention, our visualisation. The mind would say *I am not a smoker* and turn down the cigarette. The more you build this vision in your mind, the stronger the story and the easier the choice will become. These techniques have been used by elite sports coaches for years. They work extremely well. The possibilities are endless to change behaviour and I have used them from everything to improve my listening skills, change my diet and even my story with books. See, when we understand and work with the brain, it's pretty easy to have it as an ally.

Write a list of affirmations every morning and night and build the vision of a new you in your mind. Regardless of what you are trying to improve, diet, consumption of alcohol or addiction, you can create a future that exists with you not in it. Just a little side note we can remove these habits from our lives, yet the underlying cause may remain. If we are using food as a coping mechanism for a problem, we can use our new affirmation to remove the food, yet the problem could remain.

My diet now mainly consists of plant-based foods and gluten-free. I was vegetarian for a while, much to the judgement of my last boss. He still is very much of the golden era where eating meat is a must. I could see and feel the shame in his eyes when my work lunch was vegetarian. Was a great laugh the day I told him I wanted a vegan, gluten-free pizza or even worse the Friday I opted for the salad. Jokes aside, we must choose these healthy options under all circumstances. Regardless if our boss is judging us, we must pass on the office birthday cake. The removal of gluten and other harmful substances is a must if we wish to heal our minds and body.

My old boss is a great example of male culture we have built and cemented in Australia. A culture that is more accepting of unhealthy food choices than healthy. He was a great boss and an extremely intelligent man yet needed to be more aware of what was driving his relationship with food. Our perception of nourishment can go way beyond food. One of the greatest decisions of my life was to remove gluten and dairy from my diet. For years I had suffered from small amounts of inflammation from eating pasta and pizza. This inflammation was something that my body would then have to heal. The body is already working overtime in this stimulating environment. Reducing the amount of foods that are not natural to the body has had an amazing effect on my waistline, my mood and my mental focus has improved drastically.

If you are looking to up your healing, there are plenty of options. A naturopath visit will assist you on the foods that could greatly assist you in detoxifying your body. There is new specific evidence that trauma is a living memory trapped in the cells in our body. So, as we lose weight and detox key organs, we shift and release the trauma too. Our major organs are a large driving force behind our emotions. That's why breathwork and sound healing can have such a profound release within the body as we are using sound or breath to assist these cells to come cleanse. By stimulating the cells, there is a release of the negative trauma and energy stored in the body.

Let's say, for example, the body was to suffer a large trauma. In that instant, the energy present would be stored and transferred to our body. Our cells would hold on to and store this energy. So that's why we may continue to live out these feelings and emotions from the past incident in a very real way. So healthy food that allows our body the ability to *heal* and *deal* with our trauma is very important. Yet if we are drinking alcohol or bad foods, we are limiting the ability for the body to remove and process the energy from the incident. The best part about all of this is that we hold the power to listen to our body to see what agrees with us. If we use our awareness and observe our food choices, we can observe what is in alignment and what is not. Every time I ate pasta or bread, I would feel bloated for a few days. This is one of the many signs and signals our body gives us when it is not in alignment. As a soldier, we have been conditioned to *not* listen to our body, and it takes work to reconnect to this.

Our breath can be perceived as something nourishing for us, too. It makes us feel refreshed and full of energy. It can assist with creating large amounts of joy and release symptoms of stress or anger. The breath is also a great tool for breaking negative thought patterns and anxiety. When we break it down, there is nothing more nourishing in life than the breath. It is very underrated, and as a human we take it for granted. In the not too distant future, humanity will understand and unlock the potential for breath as the ultimate source of nourishment. Breathing exercises are part of my daily and weekly routine. I listen to my body and my mind when and where I need this. It is not only a great tool to help us heal from our past, but a way to stay in alignment as well.

These days I place a great emphasis on self-love too. At first, I just changed the perspective on common things I was doing to be self-love. So, if I was to choose a more expensive product because it was organic and healthier, I would see this as an act of self-love. We are all born with the ability to love and care for ourselves deeply. As we grow older, we can lose the ability to give self-love, this can be directly tied to our self-worth. We also look externally for this and think it should come from another person like our partner. This is wrong. We need the ability to love ourselves as males and to show up for ourselves. We will find the deep dark corners of our heart and our inner child need the most love. By us correcting our food and limiting alcohol, we are already showing immense self-love. These choices alone would be a great place to start in a self-love routine. By starting mediation and being aware of our own body, that is also self-love. The more time spent focused inwards or creating space for ourselves, the better we become.

THAT MAN WHO LOOKS BACK AT US IN THE MIRROR NEEDS SELF-LOVE.

Most of our anger as males comes from our boundaries that are being crossed. The sad thing as males is we do not even know the boundaries exist within. By establishing boundaries within our relationship we are giving self-love. When we consume too much alcohol and feel hungover the next day and become short and angry, our anger is generated by us crossing our boundaries. We feel a deep level of disappointment that we have drunk copious amounts of alcohol. Too much consumption, staying out too late; these are all boundaries. So, if we were to get angry at our partner for consuming too much alcohol, that is a behaviour that could be corrected. It is not right or wrong to get angry, but it is a chance for us to witness a reaction. We can then take responsibility for our reactions. We can achieve that in multiple ways, stronger boundaries on what we consume or simply not staying out as late. We could even communicate to our partner about how we are feeling and ask if they could possibly give you some time as you are feeling *not* full. The concept of not feeling full and self-love go hand in hand.

If we are not full, we must take more responsibility for how we are showing up to our relationships. By giving ourselves more love we can fill up our cup and be more present in life and our relationships. This is a positive cycle because the fuller we become, the quicker we notice when we are not. This could be seen as not being in alignment. Once we feel we are not in alignment we can redirect back to a feeling of alignment and back on course. We could also set boundaries to limit it from occurring again in the future.

Another form of nourishment is routine. Some may see routine as boring and unfulfilling. Yet, I promise you that you can find enjoyment, be relaxed and not be as stimulated in the morning to set you up for success. There is an old quote that says, 'If you don't have time to meditate for twenty minutes you need to meditate for one hour.' The point being, as we meditate each morning, we create a certain level of stillness and calmness that is mirrored out into the world. This has massive impacts on our nervous system and any adrenal and cortisol issues we have from the military. Waking up to an alarm clock and forcing our body into action with coffee is not the answer. It is an option, but this will not support us releasing any form of trauma or attachment.

My morning routine starts when I open my eyes. I start by repeating a few positive words to myself. My phone is on silent mode, and yep, you guessed it; I lay in bed and build the vision of the happy healthy me. I then take time to tune into my body. On some days when I am not feeling amazing I may share with my partner. I might wake up and feel tired, or like I woke up on the wrong side of the bed. Communication gives her the ability to understand that I may be processing something. I then drink lots of water and have a powdered green juice. Depending on how I am feeling, I would conduct a breathing exercise which includes simple forms of movement followed by a meditation. I don't drink coffee and would more than likely have a fruit smoothie for breakfast. I am not meditating at dawn, yet I ensure that I make this space religiously. Within starting the day this way we create space for ourselves. We then carry that space forward into whatever we do.

If you are a parent, try swapping days for one another and giving the other person the choice to create space in their morning. An important part of this routine is our nightly routine. I now listen to my body when it's tired and is telling me to go home and go to bed. These yawns and signals from your body are not there to be ignored. As of late, if I feel tired when out with friends, I politely apologise and go home and put myself to bed. Sleep routine can be a very large part of correcting the damage that has been done to our adrenal glands in this over-stimulating world. This same energy system that fuels our late nights out is the same one trying to process our anger and our natural healing ability. The human body has a natural ability to heal itself, yet this would not happen unless we change our behaviours.

The ultimate routine change would be to head to nature for a few weeks. If we went on a retreat in the jungle of Bali, no Wi-Fi, no phone and only natural foods, we would begin healing. We would be removed from stimulation and toxic foods. We would have a lot of downtime to become aware, no phone or artificial stimulation. It would get pretty real pretty quickly. Most people could not handle the downtime and the disconnection from the outside world. This is because in the stillness we have to reconnect to ourselves. So, the natural nourishment from mother earth and within ourselves would begin healing us straight away. It's only in these western worlds that we have complicated everything with phones, money and judgement. If it's just you and nature, your breath, the natural vibration and sound from nature, you would heal quickly.

I spoke earlier of space being a form of nourishment. In this isolation in nature and disconnecting from the outside, we reconnect to our internal world. Space is a great form of nourishment and something you should factor into your day or week. A lot of our inner child wounds relate to needing validation from the outside world. Also, PTSD and other severe traumas can see us wanting to escape or stimulate ourselves. So, if you go plant yourself in the jungle for a while, expect it to be pretty confronting at first. The short-term discomfort would greatly be worth the reward though. If this is something you feel called to do, close your eyes build the vision [... fill in the blanks]. We truly do have endless potential if we put our heart and minds to it, so if you truly wish to heal, this would be an excellent place to start.

As I have mentioned previously, life is just a series of relationships. So, it is important to make sure these are nourishing too. We are the sum of our core relationship, so make them count. You may find on this path that you need to remove yourself from some of your relationships while you adjust life to meet your new vision. This is a great positive in the end. This will allow you to not be tempted to cross your boundaries yet will also allow you to establish new relationships that are more nourishing. Like-minded people will help inspire you to become a better version of you and lift you up. The conversations will be different to those who have only known you, as you were. It may also feel like you have known them for years or a lifetime. This is exactly how it should be, and it's very exciting when you make this new level of friendship. It's like you have a common goal of wanting to improve yourself and find the real enjoyment in life.

YOUR *VIBE* ATTRACTS YOUR *TRIBE*.

Should you be negative and fixated on the past, so will your tribe. If you are drinking and gambling, so will your tribe. If you are eating plant-based foods and talking about helping one another, so will your tribe. Who we attract and the opportunities we attract are directly related to how we see and interact with the world? Ensure you are nourishing to your friends' relationships also and are here to help assist them. These days I like to look at my relationship with the world by looking at the big picture and understanding how much I can be of assistance. Just by smiling at a stranger or allowing a car or scooter to pass, we can have a positive impact someone's day. By being aware of how we spend our money we can also be nurturing to earth and our relationship with it.

This might sound like a bit of an oxymoron, but resistance can be a great form of nourishment. Discomfort can feel like the opposite of nourishment. Yet, if the discomfort has a cause or a light at the other end, it is well worth it. When we face our past or difficult situations, it is possible to change our perspective. Seeing this discomfort in another light is a great way to grow and expand. To have gratitude for discomfort or pain from the past or view the experience as nursing allows us to create a new story. A story where healing does not have to be looked at in a negative way. Yes, it can be traumatic to relive our past pain and experiences, yet this is how we come to live in our highest potential. The more positive the story around us dealing with our pain, the easier it will be. Suffering is pain with a cause. Our cause in this is to grow, expand and heal from our past experiences. So, we can view a difficult conversation with our partner as a situation to grow. A new opportunity to discuss this topic with ease and leave the past where it belongs. Even in writing these chapters, I've witnessed a lot of Army behaviour around my resistance to authority. I am very grateful for all the experiences I receive in the future that allow me to change my story around authority. Any moment can be viewed upon with a new perspective and a new story to rewrite the past.

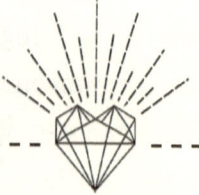

ACTIVITY: SELF-LOVE

Stand in front of the mirror and say *I love and accept you!*

Clothing is optional if you find it hard to accept parts of your body, although, I definitely recommend you bare all. Accepting yourself can help you accept the parts of your past you have locked away.

Our PTSD and trauma are still stored emotion that is suppressed and needs love and acceptance. Mirror work is very powerful!

chapter twelve
visualisation

Sports scientists have been using visualisation techniques for years. The human mind is pretty impressionable, and this is one way to help shape your own future. Like most tools in the self-improvement path, it is intention and effort. We have an intention to better ourselves; we close our eyes and build the visualisation. The effort in this part is how long we repeat this process and how often. The more real we make the detail, the bigger the pathways created in the mind to assist you to change.

Once we build a visualisation to the mind, this becomes like a real event. There is a story, thoughts, sounds and feelings that now exist in this possible future. As we strengthen this visualisation through repetition, we receive more rewards. Our mind can calculate the positives that exist in this future, too. This is very important because of the bad habits that we are trying to ditch also have a story. They are also real, yet now the mind can see they are just a quick win and cause us more harm.

So now we have a choice within the mind, two possible futures that could exist: a quick win or a future filled with positive thoughts and a healthy version of you. Without the visualisation, the mind only knows the old path and for our old habits. The more real you make that moment, and the more positive memories you anchor to it, the more real it becomes in your mind and body. Your mind will weigh up its options, long-term health or quick win. This is pretty powerful stuff and can apply to any habit or part of your personal development you would like to break or fine-tune.

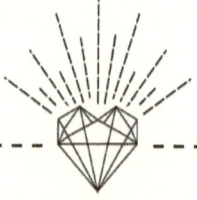

ACTIVITY: VISUALISATION

Think of something, one thing you would like to change in your life now, one habit you'd like to break, one pattern you want to stop repeating.

Keep it simple, one that you can easily imagine attaining.

Get in a comfortable position, in a quiet place where you won't be disturbed. Relax your body. Start relaxing each muscle in your body, let all tension flow out of your body.

Breathe deeply. Count down slowly from ten to one, feeling yourself getting more relaxed with each count.

When you feel deeply relaxed, imagine the thing you want exactly as you would like it.

Now, keeping the idea or image still in your mind, mentally make some very positive affirmative statements to yourself (aloud or silently, as you prefer).
"Here I am spending a wonderful weekend in the jungle …"
"I accept myself as I am …"

This statement serves as a reminder to you, and you could incorporate this in your future morning and evening affirmations.

If negative thoughts arise, don't resist them. This will give them a power they don't otherwise have. Just let them flow, acknowledge them, and return to your positive statements and visualisation.

chapter thirteen
breathwork

Breathwork releases all types of trauma. I have truly witnessed some incredible transformations in myself and others through this practise. There are multiple styles being delivered around the world today, and I would recommend nearly all. The style that has really resonated with me is open mouth connected breathing. I have completed breathwork with some amazing teachers and facilitators and would like to give thanks to all that have held space for me while I explored new depths within myself.

In connected breathing, you inhale until the upper chest and lungs are both full and release with a controlled exhale with little to no pause between breaths. From my understanding, the breath allows us to reset our body's nervous system and reset. All the fight-or-flight responses that have been left incomplete over the years have the opportunity to be released. These fight-

or-flight responses can also be referred to as implicit memories. A memory yet to be felt and metabolised safely. These effect part of our body or nervous system that still have an attachment to a past situation. If you have suffered large amounts of trauma, this can literally be viewed leaving the body. Our body may pulsate, shake or tremor as the body releases this trauma. It is very incredible to watch and experience. A large range of powerful emotions can be experienced in an amplified way during and after the breathwork. As the memory of our trauma can be stored within in our body the breath allows us to reconnect and remove this.

I have witnessed people screaming, crying and shaking uncontrollably. This is deep stuff, yet one of the main things we need to allow as males is the ability to feel. The ability to create a space where when can allow any emotion to come forward to be released. There is a possibility that you might cry like you never have before, but it is a beautiful release and something to truly be celebrated. To receive a large release of the pain we have been holding within our body is an absolute blessing.

These large sessions are something that should be conducted with a facilitator. They are trained to help you explore your body and see where the pain and attachment is stored within you. There is science showing that the body displays its trauma. So, a trained facilitator can witness your pain body trying to shift this trauma and can facilitate this within the session. After some breathwork sessions, I have felt like I have played a game of rugby. There can be times where you do not process your grief or pain in the session, and we could release these afterwards. So trying to book a session on your lunch break is not the thing to do.

Another piece of advice that may assist you with exploring breathwork is to remain open and adopt the beginner's mindset. What does that mean? Sometimes we can have an agenda our mind creates that may limit our experience. If we have a story about healing a certain memory, we may limit the ability for us to explore other avenues of our past. Remaining open can assist with all healing and also is a great intention to live your life by. When Ruth and I had left our corporate jobs, we remained open to possibilities and ended up teaching meditation at the Pyramids of Chi. Never in a million years would that opportunity of crossed our minds!

Another amazing benefit of breathwork is *space*. When we remove the pain of yesterday, we naturally upgraded our body and energy to a higher state. This higher state is where our happiness and new attitude towards life is born. Through creating this *space*, we have endless potential. This reclaiming of space can be viewed as connecting to parts of your body or nervous system you may have once disconnected from. We can create this space in our day by using mediation and our morning routine. To add smaller parts of breathwork to our daily routine can be of great assistance.

The O2 Awakening breathwork facilitators have a daily breathing practice that I have used many times to assist my morning routine and to create more space. They teach 10 open mouth connected breaths followed by holding your breath, then 20 and then 30. Just by adding a small amount of breathwork like this to our morning can have profound effects on our emotional health and how we carry ourselves through our day. We can complete this prior to mediation and allows us to connect to our higher self very quickly. Through space we create connection, and connection equals stillness. This limits the thought processes swirling around in our mind, and we connect back into our body and our heart very quickly. States that could take fifteen to twenty minutes to achieve in meditation can happen in a matter of minutes with the breath. We are altering the brainwaves existing within our mind by using something as simple as the 10, 20, 30. If you visit the O2 Awakening website, www.theo2awakening.com, you can download how to build this into your daily routine.

Many of the times on this path to heal I have just connected to my breath to breathe. It could be heart breathing or just a controlled style of breathing, its free and accessible at any time. Should you be struggling with an emotion or a thought pattern that is getting you down, we can just breathe. Just sit in your chair and breathe for 3-5 minutes. We know that we must take responsibility for our moods and correct the behaviours of the past. Even when writing this book, I have been using breathwork before I write to connect to a higher version of myself before writing. Then when I need a little break, I head outside and use the breath to recharge my energy, focus and attention.

I had the pleasure of participating in Kundalini tantra classes with Master Katut at the Ohm retreat in Ubud, Bali. Master Katut is a weapon. His flexibility and power of his breath looked like he had been doing it his whole life. He has great energy and a great sense of humour and is truly amazing to witness. His class went for 1.5 hours and included a movement-based yoga with breathing that focused on circulating natural energy that exists within our body. This was extreme and was a real challenge for my body and mind with the current state I was in. I had quite a profound release after his first class and was sore for a good few days afterwards. Master Katut's class assists us in releasing the past through the power of the breath and movement. He also includes a lot of hip opening stretches that are well known places in the body that store emotional trauma. During some styles of breathwork, facilitators would assist you to release certain parts of your body by applying pressure and massaging you to assist a release.

In Bali there is a large yoga establishment called the Yoga Barn. One of my good friends Kerry Clancey works there. She is like a mother to Ruth and me, and we've shared many laughs and beautiful memories while in Bali. She had a near-death experience and has written a book, *Heal to Live*, about spiritual wisdom and transformation. I would highly recommend paying the Yoga Barn and Kerry a visit. Another breathwork meditation that Ruth and I frequently visited was Punnu's active concessions meditation. This is technically labelled a dynamic meditation yet is no different to a breathwork session. It focuses the mediation on breathing into and observing certain parts of your body while holding hands with the person beside you.

I participated in this meditation with up to 60-70 people all joined in a large circle. The energy present in breathing and meditating in such a large group was very powerful and could be felt throughout the whole experience. I had the pleasure of experiencing this mediation several times. The releases and energy that I shifted were profound and to this day some of the most heart-opening moments I have had in my life. Honestly, it felt like every time I participated in one of his mediations, I would upgrade my heart. Upgraded by removing the attachment and the perceptions of the past to witness what was always present, love. To think that we are not love and experience love in every moment is an illusion.

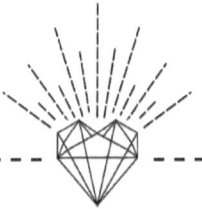

ACTIVITY: BREATHWORK

Set an alarm clock on your phone for three minutes.

Lay on the bed and close your eyes, place one hand on your belly and one on your chest, open your mouth and make an O shape. Take a deep breath into your belly and chest, filling them at the same time. Your belly should rise as you inhale, make sure your inhale and exhale are even. Ensure your exhale is slow and controlled not forceful.

The idea of this exercise is to keep your awareness in your body and explore the sensations that arise. I do this activity daily and was a large part of my healing from PTSD.

chapter fourteen
journaling

Better out than in. We have suppressed our emotions and the ability to express them for such a long time. Journaling is a very constructive way to help connect with the past, present or future. By activating both the left and right-hand sides of our brain in journaling, we can have a very simple, quick and profound release.

To break it down, get a book a pen and start writing. The more confronting the topic, the bigger the release. At first the writing might not make much sense and that's okay, its more around allowing free expression in the moment. Often that is really experienced in this modern-day and age. By doing something that allows us to express and connect to our feelings, thoughts and behaviours, we are elevating our awareness and strengthening our ability to express ourselves. Also, we can bypass our mind and connect to a deeper level of intelligence that our body holds.

We are connecting with our emotional body on a deeper level. This can go a long way in helping us express ourselves in the moment. This free expression might not sound like much, yet it is the answer to all our problems. No longer will we disconnect or suppress how we are truly feeling. In this, we connect to the body's natural ability to process the moment and not build up tension or trauma.

chapter fifteen
sound healing

When Ruth and I visited the Pyramids of Chi for her full moon in cancer—this was to be the strongest full moon for well over fifty years—we were coming from the Yoga Barn and were running late. We jumped on our scooter, and it wouldn't start. Ruth and I looked at one another and laughed. We are big believers in 'drive there slow, get there fast', so off we eventually went. On arrival at the Pyramids of Chi, Peter, the owner, greeted us with two words, "You're late."

We deeply expressed our apologies and took our seats. Just as Peter put his lips to the mic, a loud downpour of rain started. Peter's frown quickly turned to a smile. He thanked the couple who were late, us, as we'd saved everyone from being stuck in the rain. There is always a higher plan at play so when the scooter doesn't start; the lesson, just go with it.

That night was our introduction to the Pyramids of Chi and was a very powerful experience. Ubud is well known to be a place of healing. The energy and vibration experienced within the pyramids is powerful. The play large ancient Chinese gongs and other sacred instruments while 70 people lay down to receive. Our body is made up of roughly 70 percent water too. This means the vibration within the pyramid can assist with large releases within the body. The water that is vibrated within our body from the sound can assist us to remove the memory and the trauma. Sound healing exists across the country and can be a great way to you elevate. One of my favourite instruments is the didgeridoo, an Indigenous Australian musical instrument. They often played this within the pyramid and for me it makes every hair stand up on the back of my neck. Should we look at our body as energy and vibration, the didgeridoo is perfectly designed to assist this flow. Should our flow of energy be out of alignment, the didgeridoo can assist with retuning it to normal. They invited me to assist some of the gong masters in the pyramids on a recent trip. It was incredible to see the transformation that people were receiving from one sound session. There could be up to ten people per session cry or releasing anger. This is both a credit to the pyramids and the space the gong masters are holding. The gong masters are all extremely talented and have done a deep level of healing themselves. Through this connection to their own hearts and the intention and effort they put into each session, you will receive whatever you need.

The intention and vibration within sound are very important

as we heal. As mentioned earlier, our words are a window into our inner world. So, choosing our words wisely is very important. As is the music we listen to. The intention and the vibration behind the words reflect where the artist who created the music was at the time. As we heal our body, we may find that our taste in music changes and we are being more drawn to particular sounds. This is your body's natural intuition and should be listened to. If we are eating low vibrational foods and drinking alcohol, we won't be as sensitive to the music when we listen to it. Yet once you have healed and created a certain level of space, you may like your music to be more nurturing. I find Kundalini yoga music very nourishing and often listen to this as part of my daily routine.

chapter sixteen
energy healing

This is where I really made huge shifts within my healing. I was gifted one of the purest people I have ever had the honour of meeting. Beverly Dallas is an energy healer in Perth, Western Australia. She devotes her life to being of service and is the true embodiment of everything I look towards and aspire to be.

Ruth and I often joke that she does not walk anymore and floats around like a wizardess. I found Beverly by chance and had been working hard on my self-development. I'll say this now as Beverly would not like to take credit and give credit to the medicine. The energy modality ITA (Integrated Therapeutic Alignment) has been built by Beverly's long-time teacher, Melany Ryan. She is a fifth-generation healer who's devoted her life to being of service and making and teaching students like Beverly how to assist our natural energy fields in returning to what they once were.

This work is rocket fuel and I often have left Beverly's unable to fully walk and with a blissful sway in my step.

After laying on a bed for roughly an hour and with minimal contact, I normally can't operate my motor vehicle. As I said, very powerful. I normally sit in my car with a smile on my face with new levels of love and gratitude. Before I explain my limited perception or understanding of how this works, I ask you to have an open mind. Yes, what I am about to say goes against everything we have been taught but I have directly experienced the change and witnessed this.

The human body is made up of energy just like a battery, negative or neutral at our feet and positive at our heads. It is scientifically proven that walking around bare foot is good for us as there is an exchange of electrons with the earth. Melany has broken down the ancient understandings of how our energy enters our bodies and the flow. Within ITA energy medicine we can access and restore our natural flow of energy. These flows of energy for me were specifically related to blocked channels within my heart. On receiving treatment, Beverly would assist the masculine and feminine flows of energy that naturally exist within us by working with my meridians. These are like energy highways and follow the same beliefs as traditional Chinese medicine, if you receive acupuncture, they are trying to restore this flow of energy within the body. Once we restore the masculine and feminine energy from a positive and natural perspective, we can assist specific channels to remove the blocked energy. This blocked energy results from emotional pain and inherited emotional pain. At the end of the session you will receive homework to help assist the mind to reflect your new emotional and energetic state.

The homework is affirmations, specify aligned with the stories that attach to these energy blocks. Yes, you can clearly see there is a pattern in us healing the damage within our own hearts. A pattern that we are built on sacred geometry. That's the basis of how we are woven into the world as patterns of recurring energy. As I said, keep an open mind. The affirmations are very powerful for allowing us to change the fear and the lack of self-love that lives within. We dedicate each affirmation to a specific channel within our energy body. Within the heart, we have specific channels that are cleared back to our normal state. Beverly is ultimately helping us guide ourselves back home through intention and effort. This intention and effort are us calming the mind and allowing ourselves to receive what we might deem magic by today's standards. Yet we all have a natural baseline of energy. It's the accumulation of war and emotional pain and our mind that stops us from allowing our energy to flow freely. We base much of this on the mind and it is projecting the past and continuing the suffering.

It was after one session with Beverly that it dawned on me that I was in love with Ruth and did not have the courage to admit it. I had closed my heart from my previous relationship and any form of relationship seemed like a ridiculous idea. That's the resistance that I have been referring to throughout this whole book. That resistance was where all my real growth and healing would begin by choosing to love, even though it truly scared the shit out of me. I swallowed my pride and in my blissful energy induced state I had the courage to message Ruth and tell her how I truly felt. Since that day, I have chosen love and leaned into situations more painful and tragic than I have ever witnessed and experienced. Sometimes Ruth and I have had to pull ourselves apart to place ourselves and our own hearts first. Yet whenever we have dealt with whatever our projection and pain was in those moments, we have always leaned in and loved again and again.

chapter seventeen
yoga qi gong

I've also had the pleasure of participating in the Warrior Revival course in QLD, under the instruction of Master Yang, a third generational Qi Gong and martial arts expert. He is the real deal and travels the globe to teach thousands of students. Master Yang had treated a student from the Special Air Service Regiment, Jay, in 2017 for PTSD. Once Jay embraced the assistance he received from Qi Gong and Master Yang, he started Warrior Revival to assist other soldiers. Set over ten days in the hills of the Gold Coast, ex-service men and women come together to reconnect to themselves and study the art of Qi Gong. Art is the correct term and something someone could spend a lifetime exploring. To make this clear, I am a Qi Gong rookie and plan to go deeper with my practise and understanding in the future. One aim for Qi Gong is to understand the inner workings of the human body and facilitate a healthy body and mind.

Through the use of repetitive full-body movements, you can turn off the stimulation of the outside world and calm your mind. As most soldiers have put their body through the paces over the years, these movements can be very healing and assist spinal and joint alignment. I found the repetitive movements very nourishing for my spine and helped with some pain I had within my neck and shoulder at the time. With the gentle and continuous flow of the movements, you bring your awareness and attention back into the body.

In such a stimulating world, this is quite the contrast and very healing as we explore our automatic systems and expand our awareness. As the basis of Qi Gong is the internal movement, we circulate large amounts of blood and cells with the intention to heal and improve our bodies. Through the use of stomach rolling actions that include the prostate, anus, abdomen, spine, neck and head, we reprogram our cells. As we shift our cells consciously through our bodies through movement, we receive the Qi Gong magic. Like most things in life when we have a pure intention, and we put in the effort, we will receive. As we move our bodies with this intention to heal, we connect with our old cells and create a nourishing environment for our new cells. As our cells move, we send energy into motion within our body.

EMOTION IS JUST ENERGY IN MOTION.

We can witness emotion in the body and become the observer

too. Emotion is just energy in motion. This can be confronting and often unfamiliar for the modern man in this busy world. I witnessed many stories on this QI Gong course playing out within my mind and body and am very grateful for the experience and teachings from Master Yang. With Master Yang's age (60) and his family lineage comes a deep understanding of the internal process of our bodies and minds. He uses his skill and understanding to transfer his knowledge in some truly magical ways. He holds space for you to move your body and upgrade your life one cell at a time.

Coming into this course, my body was pretty banged up from adrenal fatigue and the anger I'd shifted in the last six months. So, it has been a beautiful battle and a lot of growth for me to move my body into uncomfortable situations that push me to my edge. As everyone's journey is unique, so are the transformations and lessons learnt from this 10-day course. The course is very inclusive and caterers for the odd war stories and all services.

In the stillness of the Qi Gong I could feel a deeper connection to certain parts of my body. Like I was becoming aware of the organs within my body and sensations that are not normally felt. As we connect deeper with these particular organs or body parts, we can give them more attention. In our practice, we are circulating the cells and participating in the particular movements needed to restore our cells and bodies to their former glory. When I say cells, I mean the trillions that fill our body and are regenerating every day. One of the amazing things about Qi

Gong there is no room to hide. There is not one millimetre of your body that is not explored through movement. As we know, we store trauma in the body. We are truly exploring our bodies one millimetre at a time to find the areas that need our attention.

These methods can have profound effects at removing the damage from our cells to heal PTSD and even cancer. Once we reach a certain point within our practice, our body become fluid. No longer is the mind in control of our movement. We are nourishing the parasympathetic nervous system through an automatic movement from the body. Like on autopilot, we know where and when to move to assist maximum release. This is deeply nourishing and a very blissful state. I have had some deep laughter episodes during this practice and have connected to my true state of being. As we remove the blocks of energy, we become lighter and more in line with our true self.

If we look at the human body from an electromagnetic perspective, we can see what looks like a vortex at our feet and heads. As we move our inner organs and cells, we produce large amounts of heat within the body. This heat could also be viewed and felt as energy as it moves from the inside out. In the slow movements, this energy can be felt within parts of the body. Small waves of energy can be felt from our fingers and beyond. This very ability to feel such detail at the moment is the very key to healing our bodies and minds. The more presence we have in the moment more blissful life can be as we let go of the past. This ability to feel our deepest emotions, energy, pain and pleasure can then be taken back to our lives. We are upgrading our ability to feel and be present in every moment. As we head back to our lives, we can take these upgrades to assist our presence in our busy lives. Master Yang has tailored the course to remove the roots of our problems. If we don't apply the upgrades to how we relate to our lives, we can re-accumulate our same negative programming and affect our cells.

For every day spent on this course, it was like my body was moving a lot of toxins, and I was feeling very average at times. Exhausted over the first five days of the course, I had to push my body to achieve the connection and breakthroughs. PTSD can take on multiple forms that affect our bodies and minds. My body was definitely affected, and this course was perfect timing for me to heal on a much deeper cellular level. The mind-body connection is powerful and crucial to overcoming the troubles that we may encounter with PTSD. Qi Gong has an edge here and is very similar to Kundalini yoga with the mind-body connection. We are using the breath to connect and navigate our body and mind to a higher level of inner peace and harmony.

chapter eighteen
outside world

In such a stimulating world, we have become accustomed to facing outwards. We are waiting for a possible threat that may never arrive. Our current perception of the world holds so much attachment to the past. So much so that it creates our future or warps our perception to protect us from harm. If you and a loved one have ever argued on a topic where you both feel right, well, you both are. In your own reality, at least. The mind has created your memory and perception of the same events to tell you a story. So stop arguing because you are both right.

Yet if we remove ourselves from our thoughts of perception and communicate more from a place of heart, we tend not to care about who is right or wrong or the need to have the last say. Should you react to the external world, see this as an opportunity to reflect. The outside world should not make us react and should only be seen with positivity and acceptance. Every person and experience can still be experienced with a perception of ease and joy. The problem is us when we can't see the beauty. It's not the outside world at all, it's our negative attachment to the past that is triggering a reaction and not a response.

Often as soldiers we have issues connecting back to the real world and finding peace. It's not that the world has changed, it's us. We have been stimulated and stressed to a point where we are now out of alignment. This stress and stimulation limit our ability to naturally deal and cope with traumatic experiences and the world today. This is why you will see veterans living on the street and addicted to substances. Because this is not stressful to them, as they are disconnected and alone. This is survival to them their internal mechanism to cope with any form of stress is gone. I was very unbalanced and had a hard time relating to stress and the outside world. Through the use of simple supplements to regulate neurotransmitters and vitamins I could build a foundation to assist my change. I was prescribed pharmaceuticals yet elected to take natural substances from the advice of a naturopath.

For me, any deep conversation about love in any relationship would have been strange and uninviting. This is what I would call resistance or my edge. I would feel stimulated and want to disconnect and run for the hills. The opposite of disconnection is connection, and there is no deeper connection than love. A lot of men can come across emotionally unavailable because we are. Somewhere in my past I had a story that loving someone hurt me. Perhaps there was a story about being abandoned and the fear of opening up would lead to the same result. We are naturally wired to love and share openly, yet we have lost this through past experiences and conditioning. Conditioned from our fathers and lifetimes of battles have taken their toll. We are not really aware of why we are closing down, yet we can observe it in our behaviour. The level of stimulation from the outside world is causing our fight and flight response to make us disconnect. This stimulation can cause anger, anxiety, self-sabotage; the list goes on. We must remember that this is not about our relationships or the outside world. This is about *us*. We must not project our anger into our relationships from our overstimulated state.

TO HEAL OUR PTSD, WE MUST MAKE PEACE WITH THE OUTSIDE WORLD AND RECONNECT TO OUR INTERIOR WORLD.

We must observe this resistance in the external world and take note of how it makes us feel. Paying close attention to what emotions arise is important to our healing. Through awareness, we can take responsibility and implement change by doing the work. Once we understand the emotion, we can then look back to the cause of this. I'll talk more about this in later chapters. This stimulation can feel like discomfort in the form of an emotion. Right on the edge of this stimulation, a place that feels foreign is where we receive the most growth and healing. Try to remember that the discomfort is just our mind trying to protect us from the past experience that is long gone. When we make peace with the stimulation, we see the truth. This is a second chance for our bodies and minds to process something that it couldn't. The world is a safe place, and our relationships are safe and here to help us. The trauma we hold from our deployments can rock our very core. Leave us feeling unsafe and shaken.

WE MUST REBUILD TRUST WITH OUR BODY AND MIND. WE MUST ALLOW THEM TO KNOW THEY ARE SAFE.

As we observe our minds and the relationships they build with the outside world, we may witness behaviours we do not like. This is okay and perfectly normal, acceptance of the present and the past is a large part of healing. Also, we must recognise that we are not our mind and we are not our thoughts. This is crucial.

Some trauma may cause us to live our lives in a certain way, a recurring cycle or pattern based on stimulation that is long gone. This pattern is a form of protection and can be beautiful, yet we may get a bit of a shock when we realise it was us holding on to this stimulation. As males, we are so likely to bury any pain deep within our hearts. We tell ourselves we must be strong and must keep moving forward. If we bury the pain, we are never free of its effects and must beware of the consequence. In the military, we do not have the time or the internal connection to feel this pain in the moment. It feels too foreign and something we often never fully embrace. We can be so stimulated and so disconnected that it's not even really an option to heal at the time. If we give ourselves permission to unpack this trauma, we may find that we blame ourselves. Often this anger we had been carrying for years was a choice. For every day we don't deal with the past, we are just holding on to a pain we could release. We always have a choice. In understanding, we receive clarity, which is liberating but also confronting.

As we continue to face outwards, we can observe what areas of our life may need further work. Our key relationships usually are a great place to start. Reflect and see what parts of these may need improving. If we were to witness troubles or issues in our key relationships, we have a few options. We can reflect on the past and see what role and the part we are playing in all of this. Rather than blame the other person, we could take responsibility to view our past and see if we are holding on to any attachment. We could distance ourselves from the troubles as we gather our thoughts and identify our feelings. In these early stages of healing, we can need separation and change to create a life that is more nourishing. Remember that the trouble in our relationships is more than likely resistance within ourselves.

Once we have harmony with the external world, it reflects an absolute harmony within. If we witness a behaviour in someone else that makes us angry, we could use compassion and understanding. I know as soldiers this is not something that comes easy. As men, we need to relearn compassion and understanding so we can heal our hearts deeply. Having compassion for other people and understanding they may be going through something is a real sign of maturity and emotional intelligence. This form of emotional intelligence is paramount in our relationships and life. What if we didn't even need to understand or see their point of view, and we could just give compassion and understanding to all? We still must have boundaries and know the difference of when to sit in someone else's pain or suffering. Yet it is possible to view the world with a level of compassion that understands, accepts, or even celebrates where they are at. A great way to assist this process is to think of a current difficult relationship you have. Look at their behaviour and reflect on why they may act a certain way. It is possible that your actions are triggering them. They may have had a poor relationship at some point in their life that caused them to behave in a certain way. We are now applying our newfound lens and can give the relationship compassion. Meditation is the basis of how we improve our awareness and cognitive function to achieve this.

There has been much written about life being a form of lesson or opportunity for growth. What if that outside world observation was an opportunity to change? To rise to an occasion and perhaps change some of our conditioning. I have spoken of a lot of our unhealthy masculine behaviour being passed down by war. What if this was our chance to correct thousands of years of behaviour? If we continue to do the same thing over and over is there much hope for the rest of the world. Change is inevitable.

So, this movement or shift within the way we observe ourselves and the outside world was bound to arrive one day. Why not embrace it, work with it? We see lots of data that if people are not releasing attachment to past emotions; they are becoming sick. People who are not changing and adjusting to the outside stimulation lose their health and overall wellbeing. I see poor health as a big red flag that something is not in alignment and there is a need for change. Poor health is a form of resistance and can affect multiple relationships. As we continue to ignore the signs and the outside world, we become more and more stressed. We get to a breaking point, a change point or a form of evolution. Honour this calling within you to make a change.

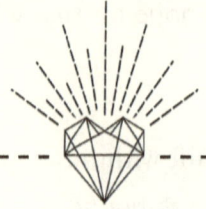

CALL OUT YOUR OWN BULLSHIT!

What are you seeing in the world that you are allowing to affect you? Our emotions and reactions are something that we can take responsibility for. Make a list of what is affecting you in your life.

Make a declaration that you are going to change this. Now, make some effort to move towards the version of you who sees the outside world for what it *truly* is.

Living through the eyes of our trauma is a choice. Yes, it takes work to change, but you have got this!

chapter nineteen
inside world

Our internal world is endless, so make sure you come up for a breath every once in a while. When we look deep within, we can understand the mechanics of our triggers and stimulation on a whole new level. As I have mentioned, the anger, pain or guilt is never about the outside world. There is something deep within us we hold on to. For everyone, what we hold on to is different and unique to us and our life experience.

When we suffer from PTSD, we can have heightened triggers. By trigger, I refer to having an internal emotional state. Often our internal reaction is not justified to the stimulation, and we can overreact. Too often we focus on the external world and what caused the trigger, it is more beneficial to our recovery if we reflect inwards. I would politely remove myself and head to a quiet room and sit and reflect. Reflect on how this trigger made me feel. Really absorb and connect to the communication and the signals my body was sending. I would then label the emotion, for me usually, it would be anger. Next, I would sit in meditation and ask where this anger comes from. If I sat there in the stillness, I would then receive clarity. I would see what I was holding on to and ask myself to release this. We can use this process for any emotion in any trigger. The time you sit with a question will vary from person to person. The process can be completed quickly once you practice it. Sometimes our triggers are not here to be removed, but to be loved and experienced.

CHANGE THE WAY YOU LOOK AT THINGS AND YOU CHANGE BY DOING SO.

I chose to heal my PTSD through holistic means and found this a way to reconnect to myself as a male. Too often as males, we disconnect from our emotions and suppress how we really feel. When we meditate, communicate and journal we can release the past, move this trapped energy that is stored within our body. That's why exercise is such a necessary process when serving in the military. It keeps us somewhat centred and allows us to keep moving. Much of my inward journey has been the story with my parents and PTSD. I believe once I worked through a portion of my inner child, then I could move on to my PTSD.

Inner child is a term given to the emotional attachment we can still hold on to from when we are children. I think a large portion of people have wounds and attachment to the past are based on the previous effects from other generations of war. Looking back at what I had inherited from my parents, my heart was closed at an early age. I guess this was lucky for me at the time because the Army needs young adults with closed hearts. My deployments and time spent in the military would send me into a downward spiral that would result in a need for change.

RADICAL CHANGE IS WHERE EVERY MOMENT CAN BE VIEWED AS AN OPPORTUNITY FOR GROWTH TO BE A BETTER VERSION OF OURSELVES.

I have cultivated stillness within. The inward and outward are closely related and all need balance for us to be in alignment. This balance and stillness are essential to return to our emotions and the ability to feel life again. I'm not saying you have to go full-Buddhist-monk to understand your PTSD. But you must apply enough intention and effort to receive the clarity from within. There you can observe and move past your attachment and PTSD. If you are on this journey already, I thank you for your effort. This can be tough, so keep up the amazing work. There will be tears, anger, guilt and shame from years of conditioning. As mentioned, these are not only ours but generations of masculine pain that need your acceptance and awareness to be released.

Each time a trigger comes to the surface to be witnessed we have the opportunity to improve. My good friend Kerry once gave me some advice, 'Just say, thank you.' That might be a hard concept to achieve at first, but it works. By just saying 'thank you', straight away you are changing your perception of the trigger and pain you may be feeling. This allows you to meet your heart and past trauma with deeper acceptance. Acceptance through gratitude is needed if you are to push through deep layers of attachment. If we meet them with resistance or judgment, we cannot shift the emotion. In every moment we truly can see the love and joy in even the deepest of pain.

If we are in a concious relationship, it is extremely helpful to give love and gratitude for our partner's emotional pain. Rather than apologising for any behaviour projected to your partner when healing, try using the word 'thank you'. By apologising we are creating a sense of separation from parts of ourselves that we are not grateful to witness. By using 'thank you' we recognise what we may have caused our partners whilst still accepting the shadow sides of our own heart. Our inner darkness can be fully seen, experienced, accepted and healed. For every trigger we work through, we release another layer of attachment to the past. Some powerful shifts can transpire in this deep work. We may lose large amounts of weight or tension and stress in our face. Our body shape may change entirely.

I know some triggers I have worked through totally changed my relationship with food. It astounded me how much of an effect my emotions were having on my relationship to food. When you free yourself from any major story, you will see how much it shapes your choices in the current moment. We truly have the power to unlock eternal abundance, joy, happiness, purpose, love and much more. All these things are omnipresent, we must just step out of our own way to fully receive them.

As the external world and the internal world become still, there is a natural guidance present to assist us. Our intuition is not something new. We know women are more intuitive. So are men, and we can listen to our inner self or higher self, all the same. This guidance and communication are always present, but we must honour the process of doing the work to strengthen our intuition. Simple examples of this are when we eat a meal that doesn't sit right, we receive communication from our body. Our body is telling us that this food is possibly not in alignment. If we do not drink enough water, this equals a headache. The list could go on and on. So, what if our body had the ability to feel that a certain person or situation was not correct and could inform us of this information? In this stillness, you can ask for clarity on where you may still be attached to the past. Many times, I have felt anger on this journey. I would sit in meditation with the simple question of 'where does my anger come from?' We are human beings with untapped potential. Einstein and Nicola Tesla were using these same methods to solve and build incredible feats for mankind.

I believe we are now evolved enough as a species to end our traumatic experiences from war. To stop the conditioning being passed on to the next generation of children. As we heal a lot of this unhealthy masculine behaviour, the past comes up to be witnessed. When we navigate our inner world, we can look beyond our PTSD and look back to our childhood. We may see the world through a perception of a younger version. That younger version of you who was wounded in some way by wars of the past. In this stillness, we can create a bond with our younger self to help them release any pain they may be hold.

We must make the time for space in our own life to receive our wisdom within. Through using meditation, we can connect deeper to ourselves. In this deeper connection we can now navigate our pain and adjust our mindset. Often when alone, I have received the intuitive answers and the wisdom I have needed to go deeper. In this intuition, often the edge will dissolve, a certain freedom or weightlessness. This can often be just a simple change in understanding or letting go of something that you did not even know was a problem. When we enter deeper into our hearts, we must take responsibility to make our own space. Space and solitude can be a form of nourishment and self-love. We must take responsibility to create every day. It is not the responsibility of our partner to keep her distance. It's on us to communicate our needs, to carve out enough of the day for our mediation and daily practice. We can then adjust this foundation depending on what we require within the flow of life. Ensure you, the observer, that your need for space is not self-sabotage or disconnecting. This is very normal inner child behaviour and disconnection and over attachment can arise when you do this inner work to free our attachment from the past.

Often on this journey, any need or want is just more resistance or attachment that can be explored. Should there be a need for more love or deeper intimacy from our partner we must ask ourselves, *where can I love myself more?* If we feel our partner is not trustworthy and we need more trust in our relationship, ask yourself, *where am I not trusting myself enough?* A want or need for something in the external world can be explored and met with love from the breath. It is an illusion that you need anything in this moment other than what is here. The new is the ever-present love that exists within every moment and can be received just by using intention and effort.

When I speak of our internal world, much of the deep healing for males is within the heart. Our heart is the spiritual centre for both male and female, yet we hold our past trauma and experiences here. Women hold a lot of their past trauma in their womb space. We must also rethink our relationship with women, intimacy and sex. We must improve our relationship with our masculinity, which will reflect how we treat women. By us disrespecting women, this is only a reflection of where we are as men. We can observe these unhealthy sexual relationships and perhaps understand where they come from. By looking at our external relationship, we can then reflect internally and understand where this disrespect comes from. I definitely had an unhealthy relationship with sex at points within my life. I am not proud of the way I treated women, but I know I had deep levels of hurt and pain within my heart that was triggered with women at times.

There was also a common behaviour of my father not respecting my mother from a young age. A child's mind fixates and remembers the negative. I also believe I would be very judgmental towards women when they were in their cycle. Rather than holding space for a woman who is honouring her body, I would label and criticise them inwardly.

On the journey with my partner, Ruth, I have learned when and where I can be of assistance and view a woman's cycle through the *we lens* as opposed to the *me lens*. As Ruth is there to assist and understand me, I am here to do the same for her. Ruth has been my greatest teacher and helped me return to my heart. The path to my heart has not been walked alone, and I have had Ruth's trust and love. To say that it has been intense would be an understatement yet suffering at times is the expansion of our hearts. I truly see the depths of this journey through a different lens and can celebrate the release of years of pain I have kept trapped within my system. These emotions of love, joy and celebration can be deeply locked away in our hearts. To access these deeply hidden emotions, we need to feel uneasy and lean into our edge of being softer. This is the natural state of the masculine and what we must return to. To heal beyond our PTSD and pain. We will grow and expand to depths we have lost for thousands of years. This is the true and modern path of reconnecting to our masculinity. Within our heart we hold the secret to accepting the world around us as we accept ourselves. For every moment we do not fully accept what is happening around us, there is a level of resistance within our own heart. We must surrender deeper into ourselves and drop in deeper.

We are born with a natural ability to communicate and be seen and heard in this world. It takes courage to rise up and break a pattern or condition that may have been with you your whole life. To stand up to your parents or siblings and speak your truth. The deeper we work on our hearts, the more courage we cultivate. We feel in alignment and grounded in who we are, which in return reflects as courage and confidence to the outside world. Should we be lacking courage, we can look within and find it. We must also remember to not judge or compare ourselves to other people as we all shine in different ways. Through this courage, we find a greater ability to be truthful. This amount of truth takes courage, yes there may be people on the way who do not understand where you are at and may get offended if you speak your truth.

Yet it is this deeper connection to our inner world where we finally cultivate a sense of who we are and when we want to express ourselves. We should always speak from a place of love and truth, sometimes that love might be for ourselves. It might mean that we need to walk away and put ourselves first. This can still be our truth. When we speak our truth with courage from within, there is no miss interrupting this. It lands, and it lands with intention. Have faith that if you receive a rejection from a loved one or friend that this is part of the process. That by you living from a place of love for self, you are now holding space for them to do the same in return. You are now a catalyst for change.

It has taken a deep level of courage to face and accept the anger that lived deep within me. Like streams of fire that could overtake me for days at a time. I needed the courage to move past the fear of not be accepted for who I was at that moment. I was always held and accepted, most of all I held and accepted myself. I was always held by my partner because she could see the radical responsibility I was making to change and to accept these hidden parts of my heart. Also, on the journey I would hold Ruth in her moments of healing. To create a space for one another takes courage. Courage to commit to something that is greater than the pain in the moment to see through the suffering that can arise. Courage to commit to one another fully with all our hearts to expose the very worst of ourselves to one another and still feel love.

To expose our deepest wounds to our partner and still be held and loved is where our love becomes unconditional. This is real *warrior work*, rockets and war is a time of disconnection and reaction to training. Once we re-enter the heart, we feel at a depth not experienced for years and release deep pain and attachment to the past. I know this part of the book can seem a bit doom and gloom, but this is a beautiful process and can be extremely joyful too. The new levels of love, abundance and joy present after these big shifts will allow you to keep showing up for yourself to heal. It will allow you to find trust in the process that you can create for yourself to take responsibility.

AS WE OPEN OUR HEARTS, WE CULTIVATE NEW LEVELS OF LOVING OURSELVES.

These newfound depths can often feel very painful and often aligned with large emotional events. In the pain and fire of what we are experiencing is our heart shifting what is no longer needed. It's a brief witness of the pain we have held. How long we sit in this is something we decide. Suffering is a choice. We are consciously choosing to lean into these depths, so the sooner we make peace with our heart, the sooner the shift will happen.

Wake up in the morning and smile and be grateful. If our first reaction is to love, to lean into our loved one and say I love you, I feel you, I know you. This is a very powerful and blissful feeling. As males, we have often lost the ability to love with deep compassion. The lifetimes of war have taken their toll on our hearts. When we listen and not dominate a conversation with our masculine behaviour, we receive. When we set healthy boundaries for ourselves, we receive. When we look at our upset partner with compassion for what they must be going through, we receive. When we see a problem and don't get angry because we can't fix it, we receive. Growth is why we are here and why we lean into and push through what we might perceive as pain. We can stay and not run from the edge of our heart. When we do, we receive more—to receive *love*. Love for ourselves to return home. When we choose love in the presence of pain, that is suffering for a cause, as there is no greater cause than to love our own hearts. As we love ourselves more, we have this new capacity to love in all of our relationships to new levels.

Union with self on the deepest level is such a beautiful thing to receive. There is a union point within you, a line where you feel the deepest clarity and an embodiment of all we have seen and been through. A final test, lesson or pattern. A point where we feel this profound liberation, a moving on. Like a new page has been turned and we are confident that we are stepping forward to a new phase. The work never stops as we must grow forever and further embody the growth we have achieved. There is always another layer and beyond this point we must venture, yet the union with self is complete. A full acceptance on the deepest level within our heart. We must move through a few layers to go this deep. A surrender to ourselves and a magic that is undeniable. The deeper we lean in the clear the journey and clearer our path becomes. There is no denying this will fill your heart with joy. We see clearly that life is a celebration and the real celebration begins beyond this point.

If you are as blessed as me to walk this path with a loved one. They will also reach this point, not through you willing or pushing, but through their own path that is deeply entwined with your everything. To be honest, the feeling to run and hide is strong, yet never reflects a fault in the other person, only ourselves. We have such deep judgement and anger for our own self that we project this from our heart to theirs. When you choose love and accept yourself in these moments, this is unconditional love for self. When you choose unconditional love for your partner in any circumstance, there is a liberation, a true feeling of worthiness and deep acceptance that goes beyond words.

This path is narrow and can seem dark without an ending but hold in there. If you have the desire to change, you will shine the light needed to reach this union within your own heart and mirror this in your loved ones. The ups and downs can be measured or viewed upon as a negative. Yet they are in the past where they belong. No longer projecting from the past to recreate our world. We have and must let these go. To be truly in the moment and view ourselves and your partner with the deepest acceptance, with every part of him or her celebrated. No flaw exists, everything always has been and always will be perfect. A connection with the world that was always present. We just have to remove our past attachment to see this beauty in every moment.

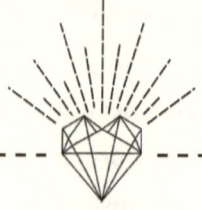

ACTIVITY: MEDITATION

Take 5 to 30 minutes to sit alone.
If you have some work that needs to be completed, finish it before the meditation.

Set an intention to let everything go, just be.

Close your eyes and connect with the breath ... *I let everything go!*

Now, I mean everything, your jaw, your stories, your need to go anywhere, the itch on your leg, the thoughts in your head. Let it all go. Relax deeper and deeper until you reach *it*—a point of stillness. You might ask what *it* is, it's that feeling is your ability to be truly present to the moment. To truly be in a state of receivership and feel how amazing the present moment truly is.
To help this focus on your breath, and repeat the words to yourself, "I let go of control."

Surrender is our greatest gift in this life!

chapter twenty
patterns of the past

As we venture deeper into our healing we see different patterns of behaviours emerging. Ultimately most of our healing is us just course correcting our behaviour from the past. We are not alone either as most people around the world act from past patterns that emerge within as well. My parents were great, and I am forever grateful for the childhood I received. As a child, I had everything I needed and more. Yet still the fear-based society founded on the wars of yesterday is still affecting children. The perception that our mother may not have loved us can shape our lives beyond comprehension. A majority of males have issues with their mother, and this is something that needs healing. We can see this in how most males treat women these days. We can then carry these behaviours and wounds into the military. Often they are the foundation of our relationship with stress and how we react to traumatic events. These behaviours that cause our fractures within the relationship may have come from our mother's father's or other masculine influences. Still originating from a relationship with the wars of yesterday. The scars that have been distributed around the world from the battles of yesterday. These scars are never a choice.

I definitely feel that my relationship with stress and my coping mechanisms to deal with stress were inherited and reinforced by my parents. Every decision from my career, money, substance abuse, partners, view on education and the outside world are all based on our inner child stories. We inherit a certain story that lives on in us, even as adults. One filled with little self-worth and little ability to receive true love. Ever wonder why you get so offended or angry at certain times in your life? Why we are triggering and have no idea? A younger version of you still lives on looking for love, to be heard, to be acknowledged.

I was at dinner with a friend last night and she spoke of a relationship cycle that had been playing out for years. When her partner become emotionally available, she would distance herself and end the relationship. This is an example of a story that can play out over and over. She was scared to be in love, scared to get hurt again. When she loved freely as a young woman, her heart was always hurt. She can see the pattern and is aware. So, when we decide to lean in, we choose love and to open our hearts again. Too often as males we are in similar situations and may not be aware.

We are here for growth and expansion and a need to evolve. We can only achieve this when we move on from the pain of yesterday. The days of playing it safe are over, we must lean into these areas and expand. The deeper we lean in, the deeper we love ourselves. It's never about loving the other person; it's loving our own heart and owning our own behaviour. Yes, I will put my hand up and say it can be confronting to do the work. Yet the ability to free ourselves from our emotions and to work through any problematic relationships is where real growth lies.

TO LIVE FROM A PLACE OF HEART IS THE NEW TREND, AND WE CAN SEE IT ALL OVER THE WORLD.

A rise of consciousness-based business and self-improvement is sweeping the globe. From food to emotional growth, it's all leading to the heart and allowing us males to grow. The deeper understanding of our inner child wounds, the deeper our healing. Our wounds to be healed live within and should be embraced and forgotten. To embrace them is to take responsibility to heal. To heal our PTSD, we must look at how we are relating to our wounds of the past. What are we bringing from the past to our current relationship with PTSD? When we are connected back to this place of the heart, the world as we know it will be transformed entirely. We're a mixture of our ancestor's DNA and lineage. I often contemplate what child patterns my parents inherited, and if that's why they married in the first place? Are we healing our own inner child wounds or generations of wounds passed down through our DNA? I will let you draw your own conclusion on that one. Yet, at times, I have definitely seen and observed behaviours from my father that can be counterproductive to who I am or the vision of myself I am trying to create. In saying that, the gifts and love I have received from both my parents are absolutely amazing. I have the deepest gratitude for both my parents and would not change a thing in my upbringing. I would not be who or where I am today. So, thank you.

We must foster a sense of gratitude for what we have in this life, we can change our perception on any behaviour we have inherited. Our DNA and family linage are in our hands now, and this is where we have the power to change it.

For us to heal our inner child world and past trauma, we must truly understand how worthy we are. At our core, we may not feel worthy of love from our parents or the world.

SELF-WORTH IS FELT IN OUR HEART AND BODY AND KNOWN IN OUR MIND.

So, make a story for yourself, one filled with self-worth, one that feels right for you. Attach it to our daily visions in the morning and repeat it aloud. Tell your partner your story, live it, embody it and believe it. We create our own stories and labels in this world, thought the power of our own minds. It is our responsibility, and the labels and stories we identify with are how we act in this game of life. We can create the most amazing story in the world and rise to a place where we feel amazing and embody this. If underneath we still have an unconscious belief of not being worthy, we must come back down and work through this. Once we have freed ourselves from our core wounds, we can truly live and be anything we choose.

Take me for an example. I have only ever read a maximum of eight books in my life. I am nearly illiterate. Yet writing this book takes me to my edge, something I am feeling called to do and something I am pushing through. I am creating a story that I am happy and whole, that I celebrate every moment. I have also built a story of being a successful author, and this book will make Oprah's Book Club. Yes, I am aiming high, but I am not attaching to the outcome and know Oprah's team are emailing me to come on the show any day now.

As I write this book, I am finding it a challenge to not sit in the old story of PTSD and my symptoms and behaviours. As I sit here and write about the past, past connections are coming back to change my story to one of yesterday. One where I am a victim, with low self-worth and a list of problems as long as my arm. So, I work harder to change my story, to reinforce the vision I see of myself in the future. I nearly didn't write this book out of not wanting to identify with the scars of yesterday. Yet I wanted to be of assistance to brothers who are healing their hearts from trauma.

We know that the mind can hold a large amount of power to recreate the past. By taking the stories of yesterday and flipping them to recreate them in a way that feels in alignment with our new story.

I recommend trying to avoid the term PTSD or try to create an acronym that has a positive meaning. That way we are working with the mind and not against it. We are now aware of what the default nature of the mind is. That we will take the pain of the past and recreate stories of blame or disconnection. You have the choice of working with your mind, to create a new story that allows you to heal and is pushing you to grow and feel great in every moment. When writing this book, my adrenal glands are not working really well and a small walk around the block can leave me feeling pretty tired. So, the story of being an author and publishing a book is something that feels in alignment. I am very grateful for this opportunity to heal and work on a project that may help other brothers with PTSD to reconnect to their hearts.

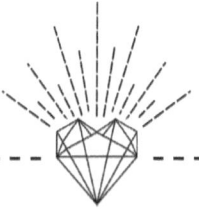

ACTIVITY: LETTING GO

Close your eyes and picture a younger version of yourself, perhaps even as a child in your mother's arms. Picture and feel the love from your mother in your heart. Know that you are worthy of this love regardless of what has happened. Picture on a deeper level you are loving yourself as a child. Know that you are safe and loved. Feel free to speak to your parents and release what needs to be said.

By communicating in this moment, we can shift attachment we may have to the past. This is some really powerful work. We may have held on to some of these emotions for our entire adult life. As we receive clarity and remove the attachment as far back as the womb, our outer world reflects our inner world. We are truly a reflection of our inner world. So, if you are always angry, depressed, anxious, this reflects our inner world and the past stories it holds.

These stories are by no way you. They are something that can be changed.

If we commit to doing the work, we can move through these quickly and have a new level of acceptance for ourselves and others.

Take a moment to look at your mother and father and witness one behaviour we are bringing to the world that we learnt from them.

The behaviour of our species 30-60 years ago is not relevant, and a lot of it is no longer serving you.

YOU CAME HERE TO BE UNIQUE. WITNESSING THE BEHAVIOUR IS THE STARTING POINT OF YOU CHOOSING CHANGE OR ACCEPTANCE!

chapter twenty-one
for the partners

For every man suffering from PTSD, there is a woman supporting and loving them through all the ups and downs and the pain. To all the women who have suffered from any war, I see you. I honour you and I say, "Please forgive us."

For as men, in these times, we truly do not know who we are. As you have seen, we've lost the way to our heart and our communication may have shown this outwardly. We are so disconnected, overstimulated and looking to escape the very emotions we need to embrace. Our fathers would hit us and tell us not to cry in tough times. Our lives have become riddled with anger, judgment and pain.

Please to all the women supporting people who are suffering from trauma, their pain and anger, this is not about you. Our pain and anger have nothing to do with you. Our pain is a projection of our relationship with ourselves. Yesterday's pain that we've buried and not dealt with is being expressed through our anger. Please be gentle with us. By loving us unconditionally, you unlock our true love. This is where the magic within any relationship starts. By accepting us, you will also have a deeper level of acceptance of yourself.

I have looked at Ruth in our worst moments and thought, *I really love this woman.* I see all of her and I love her and want to be here to grow with her. This has by no means been all rainbows and butterflies. Ruth and I have built a relationship founded on forgiveness, compassion and growth. When we have self-compassion, we can forgive over and over.

If your man appears disinterested and lost in another task, it's not that he is disconnected from you but himself. He may have elements within himself that he may not have the emotional capacity to face just yet. That's where an 'attitude of love' in every moment and committing to your partner will help him. The more you choose *not* to take his actions personally, the closer you will become. If he wants to disconnect for a time, allow him that space. He needs to feel that he is deeply supported emotionally without being judged. Love him, you now hold the key for growth within your relationship. I know this sounds tough, yet it takes a certain amount of responsibility from a woman and a partner to sit with her man's wounds.

Male and female communication can be challenging at best. It's important to communicate how you are feeling to your partner.

Not from a place of offloading or setting expectations, it's more about sharing how you are feeling within from a place of *love*. This level of communication can only effectively be delivered face-to-face hand in hand with no distraction.

On this path to healing my heart, Ruth and I have often argued and fought. Often the battles of yesterday can creep into the present moment, causing us to quarrel. It is natural to feel hurt and distrust towards a partner who can have explosive rage and fly off the hook at a moment's notice. Yet this resentment we bring forward from yesterday is not allowing us to be fully present to ourselves and partners. Ruth and I often practice meditation that allows us to remove and accept any past anger or conditions we are placing on our relationship. This is very powerful; the mind can't help but remember the fight or the hurt from yesterday.

Once someone is hurt, they want their partner to either acknowledge it or hurt too. This is where the cycle is born, and we must use our awareness to identify that our partner is needing deep love and acceptance and not rejection. Yes, our partner may be unreasonable in their comments or actions, but they are hurting on the inside and the argument is not about you. If we separate the mind and the heart, we can see that the tendency of the mind wants to even the score or even keep count. The heart just wants to love, show compassion and forgiveness. So, in meditation, we can guide ourselves from our thinking mind back to a place of heart. We can then communicate to ourselves and our mind that we accept our partner and love them for who they are. This is like conducting a little relationship reset that allows you to come back to a place of stability and love for one another. This love and stability are a more nourishing environment to heal from PTSD.

Remember, the goal of this book is to help your partner heal from PTSD and guide him back to his heart.

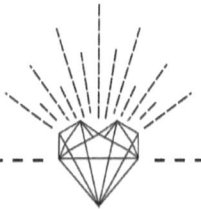

ACTIVITY: PARTNER CONNECTION

Often on this path of healing we can project our pain onto our loved ones. This can result in them receiving their own trauma and needing to protect their hearts.

Sit opposite your partner and stare at him or her in the eye. Take turns to communicate the ways you both protect your heart. Close your eyes and go back to a time in your life where you were protecting your heart. Sit in that space and feel what that felt like, now set an intention to let the walls go!

Open your eyes and both move your hands out to the side in a way to open your chest and heart to the other person. Now, breath in powerfully as your hands move out and exhale with power as your hands close in front of your face.

Do this for 3 minutes. Once completed, stand up and hug your partner with your hearts resting on top of one another.

This a very powerful exercise and something that you should definately use to supercharge your healing and your relationship!

chapter twenty-two
social responsibility

Do you answer the call to change as a male? To correct some toxic masculinity that exists within the world today? I know I have been working very hard to correct this. You might think, well, what real change would it make to the world if I looked inside myself as a male and corrected my behaviour. For the last twenty years on this planet, women have been answering the call to heal. They have done an amazing job at stepping up and breaking patterns that have existed on this planet for years. Just look at their devotion to yoga and other self-love practices. Make no mistake, men have missed the boat. Yet our healing is so deeply related. We must understand the outside world so we can better relate in our relationships. Woman must go forth to hold a space for us males to follow.

Women have been doing the work and it is now time we did. As a male heals his heart, we hold space for our brothers, fathers, friends and co-workers that a new way exists. A path filled with deep joy and gratitude and understanding. So, to all my brothers with PTSD and deep wounds, these wounds are here for a reason. They were your birthright. Your military training or traumatic events were just a divine act for you to heal deep and then hold space for your brothers. By adopting a warrior and fearless like attitude, you can go deep and free yourself. Regardless of your path, you can rise again to be healthy.

I encourage you to look at your external world and find the discomfort and lean in to do the work. Find your edge and push through the pain to grow and receive. Lean into this and your life will open in ways you have never imagined. Regardless of what you are holding, you can make one healthy choice at a time. This will result in you freeing yourself from any pain, pattern or unhealthy masculinity behaviour. You may fall down, fall off the wagon, get angry, yet as long as your desire change you can push through any edge to expand as a person. This is the real work of a warrior, and this is the behaviour that will change the world and create a new world for men to change. A world where we can freely express our emotions, learn to communicate and channel our anger in healthy ways without damaging the feminine and ourselves.

Changing our focus or redirecting our attention can be a powerful way for us to transition into this vision of ourselves we wish to be. There is a lot of negative press and media that exist in the world today. This is all fear based, and I have completely removed it from my life. I honestly struggle to even know who to vote for these days. The amount of betrayal and infighting is a large show that the world is extremely dysfunctional.

I had the pleasure of serving with a federal minister on a deployment, Andrew Hastie. He had a great moral compass and strangely grew up in the same country town as me. His past and leadership skills made him a great candidate for the Liberal Party, and he was elected as the member for Canning. I have the world of time for Andrew and in my departure from the Army he was there to recognise my contribution and hard work whilst in Jordan. He is a capable, honest young man, positioned in a broken and outdated system fuelling campaigns based out of fear. The amount of infighting between Labor and Liberal downright insulting our intelligence as a country. Andrew, if these words reach you, please form a new error in this broken leadership. Please bring forth a new version of the Liberal party and Australian politics that we can be proud of as a country. Now that's out, you can see why I place my attention on more positive and uplift content.

Google news has the ability for you to search and build your own news feed. So perhaps try adding some positive news to your day. By no means am I saying let's shun or disconnect from the outside world, yet nearly just direct our attention in a more constructive way for us. Taking responsibility for our attention has the power to change the world. If enough people take responsibility to change a new world will arise as people will shift their attention from the old to the new. The old is filled with fear and ego-based advertising, television shows based on murder and suicide. So much of our media and entertainment follows this old war fuelled behaviours.

We now know that the world is overly stimulating and causing our fight-or-flight response to trigger. If we look closely at the media and entertainment they're fuelling this and adding to the stimulation through fear. I often wonder what the stats are on people going to work because they enjoy their job. Is it possible that we work the same job that we don't like out of fear? The fear of the unknown, the fear of the transition to a new carrier that we may love. So much of our society in this day and age is based on fear and it's not healthy. Through observation, we can see that the world we interact with is based on fear. Perhaps this fear-based structure is attached to the past of war also and is something that could be changed. One might ask how we change such a large problem. It's simple, choose love. Choose what is right and feels good for you and no one else.

In that healthy choice lives untapped potential on humanity. As we choose healthy choices one after the other and shift away from the old world, we will create a tipping point. A point of change. Make no mistake, one is coming, and it will be made out of fear from the old paradigm, or from a place of love for self and growth for humanity. I predict the latter. Evolution is pretty simple. If a species can't adapt to the environment they will not survive. That's not fear, that is fact! If we observe the outside world, we can see that change must be made. We can't change the world, but we can change where direct our attention.

There is a term used in emotional development called ILOC (Internal Locus Control) and ELOC (External Locus Control), and they reference what is in our control and what is not. Internal vs external. In all the advice I have given above of the external world I have not said change *it*. I have said change your perception. It's all we can truly control. By observing the outside world and truly witnessing that *we* can change is very liberating. It's a certain level of freedom in the moment that we no longer are responsible for everything or everyone, just ourselves. I believe by me being called to write this book males are ready to change. I am not asking you to change yet, merely documenting a few dots joined from my path for you to witness. Males are ready to change, and the world needs this. The scars from war and the attachment to the past can be released. By taking responsibility, we can make this level of change required. So, when we identify what we can change our life, others can witness it with so much more ease.

I have always been a catalyst for change, in every job I would annoy my boss beyond words. Yet I never understood what I was here to change. I was always here to change myself as that's in my ILOC, my internal control. You may find on this path of self-improvement that you wish to assist your friends to change. Please take note if the information is landing with your friends. They might be an example of what is ELOC and external control. By understanding that we can better use our energy to change our internal world, we can use our energy more efficiently. Perhaps your energy is better spent on yourself rather than convincing your friends that a very new and exciting way of living exists. Sure, be yourself and answer any questions your friends might have but use your observation to see what is in your control and what is not.

The real impact for change comes from adjusting our awareness and perception of the outside world. Through doing this, we rise above any drama or negative thought patterns and lead by example. This truly is the only way to impact change in the modern world. For all the males who have amazing female partners doing the work, the jokes on us. Because slowly over time they have been loving us for ourselves, yet quietly getting on with improving their life. In this style of leadership, women are changing the world around us men. They have also been doing this patiently.

For all the women out there on their journey, I see you and I honour your contribution to the shift in the world around us today. To all the writers who have taken it upon themselves to help females rise, thank you. I would like to give personal thanks. Through your direct impact and words you have improved and held space for my partner Ruth to grow and expand. Ruth has been and still is a fucking lighthouse in my life. Shining on all the behaviours of mine that need to change. Yet without these books or your contribution, Ruth and I would likely not be in the position we are in today. So, thank you. We can really underestimate the ripple effect our change can have around the world.

A smile, a hello or just being polite may be a catalyst for change that we could not comprehend. When these amazing women wrote about their passion and healing, they may not have known that they would indirectly change a generation of men too. As we take responsibility for what is in our control, we can assist change on a large scale. It may be as simple as you posting you went to a yoga class on social media. That may have inspired someone else, and so on. By being yourself on this path, you hold space to inspire others.

ACTIVITY: WRITE FOR CHANGE

Make a list of all the relationships or places in your life that you are trying to impact change. Sometimes, the greatest change can be just simply accepting a person for who they are, in this very moment, and loving them for who they *truly* are.

I was born and raised in country Victoria, in 1985, and received some very racist and homophobic conditioning from my upbringing and my employment in the military reinforced that. This was the way of the world in Australia at the time.

My parents worked hard to build on what their parents had

achieved. Yet our household still had a lot of room for improvement. This level of judgment and non-acceptance of different beliefs is an old paradigm. The world and our civilisation deserve better. We will not grow if we continue to adopt these old belief systems. One that sees other nationalities or races as superior and man as separate from one another. We are indeed one and how we treat one another is how the world will treat us in return. Our humour within Australia has always been tied to the expense of someone else. Nothing better to talk about than to make jokes or gossip about other people. It was very refreshing to know that the other night at dinner with some friends we spoke about what our biggest challenges were and shared them with one another. That is a radical change from the old paradigm. It felt great sharing from the heart with friends about our inner world and being heard. Yes, the food was plant-based and there was no alcohol. As we do the work and improve ourselves, this is reflected in the people and situations we attract. Together we inspire and help one another be better versions together. Through listing without judgment and offering compassion for all we build a new world.

We can only take responsibility for ourselves and speak from a place of truth. I know that seeing my friends and family last year there was a certain acceptance of behaviour from me. Much to their surprise I was very different and maybe a little disappointing with my limited alcohol consumption and self-improvement talk. How do you think this would make them react? When someone they have known for years is making a drastic change, it may be easy to go with the flow, yet we have a responsibility to be ourselves. Live from a place of truth. I am not judging them or wanting them to be any different; I am truly accepting and loving them for who they are. More than I ever have before. That weekend was a great reminder to the reason I changed. It felt good to see my old friends and speak from a place of truth and the healthy changes I had made to improve.

Social media has been a big driver for me to improve. There are some amazing humans all over the world spreading similar messages to this one. It is great to find these people who share the same passion for working on themselves. We are social creatures, so walking this path alone can be a little lonely. Knowing that your heart and others around the world are following the same process to heal is a big deal. By searching for certain hashtags on social media, we can change our news feed overnight. We can mute old friends, or we can even delete them if we feel they are not in alignment. Filling our news feed with positive, world changing content can help us feel better. Sometimes we are not always sure about how we will fill in the blanks of this vision we created. That's where social media can really assist in our healing if we remain open. We must flow with life and allow the world to work its magic.

Social media is a great way that we can connect with people and workshops at the correct time. If we set the intuition to heal and make the effort to pick healthy choices in every moment, the rest takes care of itself. No plan, just awareness of what is and then setting our intention in a way to take action. Social media can assist as it allows us to pivot, to be inspired to change our direction. By interacting with social media in a healthy manner we can connect with other people's passions and purpose. This is really powerful stuff. Over thousands of miles, you can connect with people all over the world.

Together we are creating a web of change across the globe based on passion, love and healthy choices and social media is the platform. If we agree that all things in life must be balanced, there must be a balance for the internet and social media coming soon. I truly see a wave of positive influence from social media making a significant change in the next few years. For all the bloggers out there, thank you for your effort and positive change in the world. We know that the number of likes you have been not from the bases of greed. We truly see you want to help the world and playing your part to spread your message. If you are not aware of these people, I suggest you add them to your newsfeed and weave their knowledge into your stories. They share powerful messages that come from the same place as this book does. Collectively from a place of truth and authentically, we can work together to be ourselves. From this authenticity, we can assist our brothers and connect with people on deeper levels than before.

Last ANZAC Day, I was about to comment on a friend's picture. My default comment or conditioning was to make a poor joke. But on observing my comment, I was going to shame this person. The humour that was once acceptable, the humour I had grown up with and laughed at 1000 of times before, was no longer appropriate. I had to check myself and the connection I had to this old paradigm of humour, delete the comment and start again. I felt proud of myself that I could see this behaviour and correct it before I had possibly shamed my friend. So, when I speak of healthy masculinity, this is what I am talking about. They don't have to be large changes. I can still connect with my friend and comment on his ANZAC Day picture and comment from a place that's in alignment with me.

As we align with our higher self and return to our heart, the world flows in a way that we have never seen before. There are many people on this path looking for a purpose and their life mission. Your life mission is something that will always grow and change as you do. Yet as we return to our heart, we can no longer avoid our purpose in life. When we co-create from a place of love with our partner and the rest of the world, we are in a deep form of alignment and our purpose will flow. For me, I had never written a book, yet I could not ignore the calling and downloads I received to create this book.

This is me taking responsibility and creating a book from my heart. If you'd asked if these words and passion existed in me twelve months ago, I would have laughed at you. But I am gladly devoting my time and energy to write about my experience with PTSD and returning to my heart so I can be of assistance to other brothers. Throughout my path of healing, I'd always received a certain level of release when writing and sharing my experiences on social media. These words were part of my medicine. This book is medicine from my heart to yours. I look forward to assisting more brothers on their journey and helping coach them back to their hearts to find the joy in their life once again.

chapter twenty-three
shame

Shame is everywhere in the modern world. You may know this, you may not. Should you have been on such a disconnected path as I have you will have a strong relationship with shame. Yet as we disconnect from our feelings through service, or a length of time in our chosen profession, we can also disconnect from shame too. We can feel deep shame for our actions, our feelings, our sexuality, race, looks, our body and the list could go on and on. We can even feel shame for somebody else's actions.

Shame is an emotion tied to a story that you are *not* a good person deep within. So as we engage in self-sabotaging behaviour, we reinforce our story we are a bad person.

Brother, let me say this now, there is no such thing as a bad person who walks this earth, we are all just a by-product of our environment.

Yes, we can label behaviours as good or bad when we compare to social constructs and what we have been taught growing up. If you have been deployed overseas and spent time at war, there may be a part of your unconscious mind that feels shame for your actions. For us to truly heal from our past, we must release all parts of us that are still attached to any shame. The tricky part is how we move through shame and release this deep story of not feeling like a good person. We do this through compassion. Yet as soldiers within the Army, it may have served us to turn off our compassion. To turn off our love and to turn off our empathy. These emotions are automatic, no different to a sneeze or a cough, they are something that happens when the right environmental conditions arrive—they activate.

As we spend long times in service, these feelings can distract us from being our very best in our duty. We can even feel shame when we don't feel these emotions present any longer. We can reinforce our story of shame through not feeling and also through feeling large amounts of anger. Our lives have been conditioned to find anger as a negative emotion and something we can feel deep shame about. Should we have large amounts of suppressed anger within our system when we display this, it can often be labelled as unhealthy or explosive. Until we accept the way of compassion, our feelings and reactions will always be *waiting* to be released. The acceptance process for me has gone like this: acceptance, love, compassion.

If you have just started your healing journey, first, you must accept a more logical acceptance within your mind. For the human mind to *not* label something as bad and to accept actions or emotions can take work. One step further and for us to show love to emotions and actions can take even more work. Often our capacity to love ourselves can be blocked via our shame that we hold. So, working on your capacity to love again can take time. Our ability to love is also something that is automatic and something that can be activated again should we have lost touch with how to do so.

So when we apply intention and effort, we can truly connect back to our hearts and our emotions once more. It is no different than going to the gym. We can all pick up a weight and lift it at first. Some are stronger than others, but we are all unique. As we lift time and time again—applying more time and effort—we strengthen this automatic function that we have in our body. When we leave the gym and do not use these muscles for a time, they then lose their strength. The same thing can happen with our emotions, and they simply just need more intention and effort to be felt. For me, meditation, and my partner, have been the catalyst for me to feel more deeply.

I would often sit in meditation and picture my partner before my eyes and sit in the emotion of love or compassion. Should I have activated an emotion, I would then give this emotion to myself. There is an epidemic of males around the world that have disconnected from their love and if you are reading this and know in your heart this is you, it's okay. You are not alone. The first thing you can do is accept this and then give yourself some love and kindness. That's because any path on this earth walked that has disconnected you from your own love is one that should be given compassion. This is the very definition and reason why you should give yourself compassion and to stop taking on any more shame in this moment.

HOW WE DO *ANYTHING* IS HOW WE DO *EVERYTHING*.

Should you not feel large amounts of a shame, or know how to tell if you're shaming yourself, consider this. At any moment in your life that you feel like you have let yourself down, crossed a boundary, told a white lie, told a large lie or eaten or drunken something you know may not be the best for you. That is shame showing up. Know in your heart, mind and in every cell of your body you are a good person and you're stepping up in life to be the person you know you can be. Only when you can fully love and accept this behaviour from the past, can you be free of it.

Start small and release the shame you may have attached towards small things throughout your day. Then when you feel called to go deep. Go the deepest you have into your heart ever! Go so deep that you leave no stone unturned and leave no walls or barriers around your heart. Forgive yourself for every action you have ever doubted yourself. The longer you sit in this compassion, the more you will recreate this emotion in your life. Soon you will have new depths of compassion for the people and your environment around you.

If you have been deployed, worked in emergency service or any environment that has you not feeling love within your heart, I am sending you my deepest compassion in this moment.

I am sending you acceptance, love and compassion through every pain and every struggle I have ever felt on my journey. I say, thank you for your courage and thank you for your warrior-like effort to feel into your heart.

> Brother, the world needs you with your heart beaming out of your chest.
> Brother, the world needs you to feel the deepest love for yourself and others.
> Brother, the world needs you deeply connected to your own power.
> Brother, the world needs you to release your shame to help other brothers to rise.
> Brother, our hearts are deeply connected—my shame is yours.
> Together we rise.

Depending on your level of pain and suffering you have experienced or inherited in your life will depend of the level of discomfort and effort you will need to invest into your process. Remember that you could be holding lifetimes of trauma and life will test your ability to be compassionate for whatever comes up. Yet if you hold love in your heart and resist the stories of your mind, you can accept even the deepest pain that needs love and kindness.

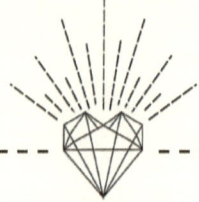

ACTIVITY: ON COMPASSION

Find a quiet space. Sit and bring up a memory of the past about compassion. It may not be, but go with it. Sit in this feeling, in this memory, in this vision, in this thought, whatever it may be, and allow it to grow through your attention.

Should this compassion be outwards focused, when you feel ready to bring this back to your own heart and sit in your own feelings of compassion. The deeper you go here, the more it will grow.

Should you feel disconnected from the world, your loved ones, and your own heart, practice this every day. Allow your body to activate these automatic systems within your body.

Should your progress be slow, please do not feel shame and do not feel guilty about your ability to not feel certain emotions at certain times.

chapter twenty-four
embodiment

If we don't apply what we learn in this life, we are missing the point. With the wealth of knowledge that exists around the world and within us, we must apply this to shape our future and the world.

WE CAN'T CONTROL THE OUTPUTS OF OUR BEHAVIOURS, JUST OUR INPUTS.

By this, I mean reactions will happen and this is the output we can't control. Yet we can take greater responsibility to control our inputs. By eating healthy foods, practicing meditation, doing Qi Gong, saying our affirmations, using visualisations, journaling and yoga, we can control our outputs. This *all* requires intention and effort. The more intention and effort we take to break our patterns of behaviour we will change. Through effort and determination, you can and will rise again.

As the old saying goes, the application of knowledge is power. So to meditate and change our state of mind and then not apply this to the real world we ask have we really achieved our maximum growth. Yes, we will improve with meditation alone, yet to really apply our knowledge we must make an intention and put in the effort to change how we are relating to the world. For example, if we were to meditate and then have an outburst of road rage, are we really applying our knowledge?

We need to take greater responsibility to change our internal dialogue, focus on our breathing, and use positive affirmations. This is us stepping up our input to match our new intention for change. So, when we break it down, we can control our output by setting up our inputs. You may wonder if it's really that big of a deal you get angry in your car. But every time we get angry, we are limiting our ability to heal. We are also affecting our levels of cortisol within our bodies and minds. It does matter. You matter. The world matters.

IN EVERY MOMENT WE CAN MAKE PEACE WITH THE EXTERNAL WORLD TO ASSIST OUR HEALING.

By making a list (journaling) of all the destructive behaviours or moments of anger, we can then set an intention to improve these. By observing (mindful meditation) our negative reactions and behaviours and then applying our attention, we will improve our relationship with the external world. If we can then remove the label of destructive and meet this behaviour with acceptance, love and compassion, we can truly transform. Often when we dive deep into resolving our behaviour, we find that the root cause belongs deep in our past. By setting the intention to make peace with our external stimulation, the path will lead us back into our internal world to do the work and remove the attachment. Avoidance is a large part of our unnoticed behaviours. Should you avoid intimacy or the softer side of your heart, you are avoiding a great power within. As a male, our power lies within our balance and our ability to tap into our softer sides. Often compassion is an emotion we avoid. These softer traits hold space for our partners, children, and ourselves to show compassion for *all* people under *all* circumstances.

Life is about balance. To embrace all sides of our heart and our male structures, we allow ourselves the birthright to receive beyond our wildest dreams. The deepest acceptance, joy and bliss are all present within this lifetime should we do the work. To embody the knowledge, we learn on this path is the gateway to our true power. In this power, we can align with our true purpose and manifest our deepest desires. If you break it down, it can be as easy as this: make the healthiest choice you can make in *any* present moment. If you feel that in reflection, you could have made a better choice circle back and work on your inputs that led to your decision in the moment.

Often on this journey, I have been coasting through and notice I'm not fully in my joy. I'm not angry or sad, just in a state of neutral. I have now found that this is an indicator to go a little deeper and reflect on my internal world. Embodiment can be explained as a responsibility to find our true state of joy. For every enemy, we hold within our life without understanding the internal projection we need to go deeper within. This takes courage to do the deeper work within our own heart. As with most anger we attract within our lives, we are really the ones who are protecting our inner anger. We must pause and reflect and take responsibility. Our natural reaction will be to blame or remove ourselves, but we can take a deeper responsibility. Imagine if the world took responsibility for all negative behaviour and anger displayed. This is the reality we may live in one day if we all play our part to level up. To remove our attachment to the past and embody the true joy that lives within each of us and our own heart. The generations of tomorrow would feel the harmony of a stable family unit living from a place of heart and not from a place of fear having profound impacts all over the world. A world founded on compassion, truth and not fear and greed starts with you.

To awaken, take control of your life from the second you wake up. Take back control of your mind and think positive thoughts. Say your gratitude aloud and feel this deep within your heart. Build a visualisation of what you want to achieve for the day. Sit up in bed and rest your eyes, do some light breathing activities and then meditate for just a small portion to start your day. Connect deeply with your body and feel your joy. Smile as you walk to the kitchen, make a cup of lemon water or greens juice. Make the intention to show your body love with this choice to not make a coffee every day. Walk outside, place your feet on the grass, move your body, Qi Gong or Kundalini Yoga would be ideal. Connect deeply with your breath and feel your body and energy in the moment. This is an example of a morning routine that would nourish your body and set you up for success for the day! This would assist you in making healthy choices for your growth mindset.

Becoming the best version of you may seem like a lifetime away, start small, step-by-step. Build a vision, say a positive affirmation, download a yoga and meditation application for your phone. Call a friend and ask for help, get a personal development coach to help you change your mindset. For every day you do *not* lean in, you are slipping further away, more disconnected and heading in the wrong direction. Think about your life twenty years from now and what it might look like. Now, imagine being depressed, angry or using the same coping mechanism for the next twenty years. It's a scary thought! Doing this work I write about is easier than staying small and battling on for another twenty years.

You deserve joy and to live a life of happiness. In tough times, use this picture as your power to make the changes within your life. Let the fear of the future drive you to be healthier. Put down your beer, turn off the television, stop blaming everyone else and take some fucking responsibility to change yourself and the way you see the world. Have faith. We got ourselves into this mess and we sure as hell can get ourselves out. You don't need all the answers on how to improve. You just need to take the next step towards a healthy choice—one after the other after the other—and the rest will take care of itself. With each healthy choice a door will open leading to another door and another door until one day you look around and say, *I feel pretty fucking amazing right now*!

CHOOSE LOVE IN EVERY MOMENT FOR YOU AND FOR OTHERS.

afterword

Often on this path it feels like I have taken two steps forward and one step back more than I care for. But often the step back is so necessary to adjust our direction. Healing wounds and the trauma of yesterday is not linear and is different for everyone. As we move towards the healthy version of ourselves, we may experience large changes in our life. This is necessary and the greatest change is often on the other side of our darkest hour, so hold on and have faith.

I can promise you if you are moving towards the best version of yourself and making positive change, your pain is just temporary and there to show you something that needs to be witnessed. Like a snake shedding skin, we can't sit there and peel a snake. Only when its time will the skin be shed.

We all have a story and on this path I have met

many brave brothers that are walking the path to improvement and truth. Thank you. I know the path you walk can seem lonely at times and like hard work. I appreciate your effort, your commitment to be a better person, and your service to want to help your fellow brothers be the best version of themselves. Should you require assistance on this path, ask for help. This would be the greatest advice I can give you. There is no higher power on this earth than to ask for help and open our hearts and minds to receiving what we need. It may not always be what we want, but it will help us grow and return *home.*

To all the old diggers out there that went to hell and back, thank you for your service and your courage. I still can't comprehend the level of suffering of the past. I believe that is a credit to how far we have come as a society to not even comprehend the wars of yesterday. You may not view the world with the same level as optimism yet. But the beauty I see and feel in every moment is just a reflection of the pain I have gone through to come *home to my heart.* Just as you will, brother.

From my heart to yours, good luck.
Matt

thriving warriors

Thank you for showing up, doing this work and sharing these pages with me. It would be an honour for us to continue the healing journey together.

Matt has built a number of online courses filled with great content to help you grow and expand, through using multiple techniques.

This course is for any man that is looking to thrive and can be found at:
www.thrivingwithptsd.com.au/warriorswar-course

about the author

Matthew Bruce is a former Australian soldier turned meditation teacher and facilitator. With deployments to Afghanistan and with the special forces, he struggled to integrate back into society and suffered from PTSD for several years.

Matthew's words and teachings are from the heart. He combines several self-taught quantum visualisations and meditation techniques to help you upgrade your life and take back control of your inner and outer worlds. Matthew has tried a vast range of holistic healing practice to heal from PTSD. He shares his understanding and experience with freely available healing techniques and how they relate to soldiers and first-line responders.

Matthew now teaches meditation and breathwork to other soldiers and first-line responders. His intention is to help other victims of PTSD understand the steps they can take to improve themselves on the daily. Through implementing small changes and taking radical responsibility for our own state of mind, we can grow deeply and move through the trauma of the past. This will allow us to remove the anger we still hold on to and move forward with our lives.

Once we understand how our minds are relating to the stress and stimulation of the outside world, we can use simple proven daily practices to create a truly limitless life.

Keep thriving and stay in touch.

You can find additional resources that correspond with the topics of this book at:
www.thrivingwithptsd.com.au/warriorswar-resources

Connect with Matt on Instagram:
www.instagram.com/thrivingwithptsd

Find Matt on Facebook at:
Thriving With PTSD

www.ingramcontent.com/pod-product-compliance
Lightning Source LLC
Chambersburg PA
CBHW030255010526
44107CB00053B/1719